A Dictionary of Bullshit

A Dictionary of Bullshit

Diane Law

Magpie Books, London

Constable & Robinson Ltd
3 The Lanchesters
162 Fulham Palace Road
London W6 9ER

This edition published by Magpie Books,
an imprint of Constable & Robinson Ltd 2008

A copy of the British Library Cataloguing in Publication Data
is available from the British Library

ISBN 978-1-84529-767-1

Printed and bound in the European Union

1 3 5 7 9 10 8 6 4 2

Contents

Introduction	1
Dictionary	3
Bullshit Job Titles	54
More Bullshit Job Titles	80
Yet More Bullshit Job Titles	109
Even More Bullshit Job Titles	146
Bullshit Builder I	153
Bullshit Builder II	154
Bullshit Builder III	155
Bullshit Builder IV	156
Bullshit Builder V	157
The Art of Sales Bullshit	159
The Art of Mission Statement Bullshit	165
The Art of Interview Bullshit	169
The Art of Body-Language Bullshit	175
The Art of Retail Bullshit	181

Introduction

Nearly 80 per cent of office workers have admitted to using "buzzwords" in order to keep up with colleagues, without having a clue what they mean. That means that there's a whole world of people out there using buzzwords to communicate with one another, with none of them having a clue what the others are on about. On the other hand, there is also a handful of people who not only use the words contained in this dictionary, but also claim to know what they mean.

Help is at hand, though, for that 80 per cent baffled by bullshit, buffeted by buzzwords from every side. If you count yourself among them, you'll find all the help you need right here, from an explanation of what "at the end of the day" actually means (nothing at all) to the meaning of "zero-sum game" – and not only will you discover what that tiny proportion of knowing buzzword-users imagine they're saying, but, for your added benefit, you will discover what they are, in fact, saying. And (an even higher percentage here) nine times out of ten that will be just about nothing at all. So, you will be empowered to sift the wheat from the chaff, to throttle back and coast, taking in only those parts of memos, e-mails, speeches, PowerPoint presentations and so on that actually mean anything, and you will be able to switch off to the rest, free from anxiety.

This is a book for anyone who has ever sat in a veal-fattening pen of an office cubicle, biting down on a pencil in an attempt to stifle rage while staring goggle-eyed at some new, meaningless profanity shimmering on the monitor: a message from the boss, perhaps, with some gibberish appended in the guise of a motivational message, or some incomprehensible instruction to do something "with a sense of urgency" – but what, exactly?

At the end of the day, however **passionate** you are about your work, however committed you might be, you run the risk of being stabbed in the back by a colleague in the course of a challenging assignment. But . . . **drill down**, and discover the **win-win**. **Change is good**, and hopefully you won't confront a **hiring freeze** as you **ramp up** your efforts to find a new job with a renewed sense of urgency.

Don't be left **out of the loop** when it comes to office bullshit!

24/365 *adjective*
absolutely no personal life allowed, especially loyalty to anyone/thing outside the company.

24/7 *adjective*
1. round-the-clock availability to your boss. 2. the impossibility of having a family, a relationship, or even a pet that might ever need your attention.

360-degree appraisal *noun*
1. criticism in the round. 2. an attack from all sides.

AAA-rated *adjective*
1. highly rated by those with vested interests in close business relationship with current owners. 2. borderline worthless.

accountability management *noun*
no one is in charge; everything is run by a large bureaucratic rule book.

accountancy *noun*
the art of lying, in a dull manner, using lots of numbers and charts.

actionable solution *noun*
a solution that can be "actioned," i.e. put into practice (as opposed to a solution that is impracticable, and is, in fact, no solution at all).

action item *noun*
1. something nobody else is prepared to do. 2. a veiled attempt to make a terrible job seem very important when everyone knows it's a pointless task.

added value *noun*
1. an upgrade on something without value, possibly in the form of something useless offered for free. 2. a form of selling a **product**/project by pretending that it is multi-purpose and works in many imagined areas.

advertising *noun*
1. lying. 2. exaggerating. 3. attempting to sell a **product** by telling the unvarnished truth (an advanced strategy, usually only attempted by an advertising executive on the verge of a nervous breakdown).

aerobicized *adjective*
1. describes a project that must be done at super-speed, possibly at the expense of food, drink, and sleep. 2. a neurotic approach to something (toned by aerobic exercise).

aggregate *verb*
1. put together several different elements, usually pointless on their own, in order to raise their value. 2. sum up the performance of a group of people when no one individual is prepared to shoulder the blame.

alignment *noun*
1. a state of agreement or co-operation among persons, groups, nations, etc., with a common cause or viewpoint. 2. the makings of a multi-national corporation. 3. misleading description of the separate parts of a misaligned company.

anecdotal evidence *noun*
1. evidence in the form of an anecdote, or hearsay. 2. the complete absence of evidence which would support a chosen course of action; the attempt to cook some up to give the appearance of understanding what is going on.

application *noun*
1. *computer science* a computer program with a user interface. 2. dedication to a particular task, e.g., "She showed particular **application** in trying to fathom the new **application** on her computer, but without conspicuous success."

architect *verb*
design and make something (a program, a system, or an approach to a task) and feed one's ego at the same time: "I am the **architect** of this." ("I think I am some sort of god.")

architectures *noun*
a system of approaches to certain tasks that has been brought about by someone who needs to have absolute control over others. See **architect** *verb*.

asap *adverb*
1. get on with it now or you're fired! 2. "Please do this now because I should have done it months ago."

aspiration statement *noun*
1. a personal account, on approaching a new job, of one's expectations, personal and professional goals, and strategies to achieve those goals. 2. a tissue of lies, half-truths, and meaningless platitudes – a collation of the applicant's apprehension of what the prospective employer would like to hear.

as we speak *adverb*
1. you should not be here talking to me. 2. a paranoid and delusional term used by someone who believes the world is against them and is continuously seeking their downfall.

at the end of the day *adjective*
1. towards evening (obsolete). 2. in truth, this means absolutely nothing, a meaningless tag appended to just about any statement to suggest that some kind of summing up is being offered. 3. a "tell" that the speaker is lying ("**At the end of the day**, this isn't about you . . ." It *is* about you.)

at this moment in time *archaic cf.* **going forward** *adjective*
1. right now, at this very instant. 2. a meaningless "tag", the archaic form of **going forward**. (Compare "We are selling 200 litres of WonderJuice a month **going forward/at this moment in time**" with "We are selling 200 litres of WonderJuice a month.")

audit *verb*
1. sign off without adequate examination (applies to companies in which you have shares or other interests).
2. scrutinize with the fearsome indefatigability of the Spanish Inquisition (tends to apply to your own company).

authentic *adjective*
1. completely made up; false; pretend. 2. substandard or defective, thus only acceptable to the marketplace if branded as authentic.

B

B2B *adjective*
1. business-to-business (**B2B**) is a term commonly used to describe the transaction of goods or services between businesses as opposed to transactions between businesses and other groups. 2. a stitch-up deal – your job is not safe.

B2C *adjective*
1. business-to-consumer (**B2C**) describes activities of commercial organizations serving the end consumer with **products** and/or services. 2. usually denigrates consumers as stupid and willing to hand over cash for pointless items or services.

back-end *adjective*
1. refers to the end stage of a process flow. 2. a behind-the-scenes action or behaviour that is hidden from the consumer, and can be lethal. 3. the programming behind the web page you are using which is collecting all your

information for its own future use, without your knowledge or consent.

backward-compatible *adjective*
usually not, in fact, but the fantasy that your brand-spanking new computer (or whatever) will interract seamlessly with your creaking ranks of ageing peripherals (or whatever it is you haven't been able to afford to replace).

balance sheet *noun*
a work of fiction listing over-valued assets and under-estimated costs.

ball park *noun*
1. a large structure containing a baseball diamond and huge concrete stands filled with seating. 2. a very rough estimate indeed – you could be right there in the middle of the pitch, or you could be in the last row of seating way up at the top of the stand. In general, a **ball park** estimate is one so vague as to be entirely useless, which a salesperson will take as completely reliable and therefore close several million dollars of business on the assumption that it is accurate.

bandwidth *noun*
1. a data transmission rate; the maximum amount of information (in bits per second) that can be transmitted along a channel. 2. "time", as in "I'm sorry, but much as I'd like to, I simply don't have the **bandwidth** to take on this particular task."

barriers to entry *noun*
1. the inability to gain access to or engage with something or someone. 2. a deliberate act by someone else to keep you in your place, outside.

base level *noun*
1. the lowest level. 2. what remains when the starry canopy of wishful projections has been stripped away. 3. the truth of a business's predicament.

battle plan *noun*
1. a plan for conducting a battle. 2. a technique employed by a paranoid person who doesn't actually want an argument out in the open, but would rather undermine his or her opponents behind their backs.

bear *noun cf.* **bull**
person of a depressive mindset, permanently expecting prices to fall, and gambling unsuccessfully on this outcome. The bear will feel personally vindicated by a stock market crash no matter how long it takes to arrive, and will regard any small fall in prices as a moral correction in an insane world.

bear trap *noun*
a temporary dip in prices, followed by an unending climb which serves to further depress those **bears** who sold prematurely, in expectation of an imminent crash.

behavioural competencies *noun pl.*
1. basic attributes such as analytical thinking, emotional intelligence, **customer service orientation** that make employees competent (or, more often, incompetent) in their roles. 2. personal idiosyncrasies yet to be crushed to nothingness by the corporate behemoth.

benchmark *noun*
1. a notch on your desk for every occasion on which you've been hauled over the coals by your boss during an

appraisal. 2. a meaningless measuring point for pointless productivity.

benchmarking *noun*
1. also known as " best practice **benchmarking**" or "process **benchmarking**" – measuring a business's practices against the best ways of doing things within a particular industry. 2. the display of the carrot before the wielding of the stick. 3. the corporate equivalent of waterboarding.

best of breed *noun*
1. title given to a dog or bitch which has been judged best representative specimen of its breed. 2. **best-of-breed** *adjective* an integrated system from an individual vendor, rather than the best individual components from various sources ("a **best-of-breed product**"). 3. a dog's breakfast of a system, cobbled together from various disparate bits and pieces.

best practice *noun*
the best way of doing things (note that this does not necessarily have any effect on quality; **best practice** may still produce worst **products** and services).

big picture *noun*
1. a view of an entire situation or issue. 2. often prefaced by "the" in a desperate attempt by bosses to get their workforce to actually do some work. 3. the perceived end result. 4. an attempt to distract attention from a localized screw-up by appealing to broader, or global, conditions.

Big Win *noun*
1. a crushing victory. 2. a blockbuster product or service which will enable a business to make a killing.

bioresponsible *adjective*
1. responsible business practices with regard to the environment. 2. being seen to care.

biosustainable *adjective*
1. ecologically ethical business practices which will sustain the health of the planet, rather than damage it. 2. business practices marginally less likely to do irreparable environmental damage.

BlackBerry *cf.* **CrackBerry** *noun*
1. "a wireless **e-mail** solution for mobile professionals." 2. a cybershackle, yoking you to your employer and **customers**/clients right around the world **24/7**.

blamestorm *noun/verb*
1. method used by a gushy boss trying to get you to work yourself into the ground for them. 2. a brainstorm to determine which scapegoat to blame. 3. to attempt to redirect blame away from oneself. 4. the dust storm stirred up by the struggle to point the finger on the one hand, and avoid being fingered on the other.

bleeding edge *cf.* **state of the art**, **leading edge** *noun*
1. a computer science term for technology which is so new that users are required to forgo degrees of stability and productivity in order to be able to use it. 2. **bleeding-edge** *adjective* an **upgrade** on **cutting edge**, which, in a previous, less macho business environment, was regarded as adequate (a **bleeding edge** is the **cutting edge** of the **cutting edge**).

blirt *verb*
1. to harrass someone by sending suggestive messages to their **BlackBerry**. 2. to try to drum up business by sending ass-licking messages via a **BlackBerry**.

blirting *noun*
flirting by means of a **BlackBerry**.

blog *noun*
1. an acronym for Boring Loser Of Grand-design. 2. an abbreviation used by journalism drop-outs to give legitimacy to their shallow opinions and amateur photography/film-making/music-making which seem permanently stuck on the first draft.

blogebrity *noun*
someone who gains notoriety from a **blog** by writing fiction in the guise of autobiography, for example, pretend call girls, celebrity party-goers, porn stars, and musicians.

blogged *adjective*
descriptive of a trivial or largely inconsequential topic put onto a screen.

blogger *adjective*
a term used to describe anyone with enough time and sufficient narcissism to document every tedious moment of their grimly uneventful lives.

blogging *verb*
if minds had anuses, **blogging** would be what a mind would do when it had to take a dump.

blogging community *noun*
a loose association of the under-employed, the lonely, and the mentally ill.

blogomania *adverb*
thanks to certain internet sites, we're all doing it now.

blogosphere *noun*
the **blogosphere** has replaced the information super-highway as a term for the place where one will find no useful information whatsoever.

blogroll *noun*
an interminable list of links, none of which anyone will ever click on.

blogshare *noun*
an imaginary shared collection of a **blog**'s worth, which is ironic, since most **blogs** have an imaginary share of readers.

blogstorm *noun*
an unquantifiable mass of people uploading their value-less, though strongly held, opinions on the internet at the same time.

blog swarm *noun*
a **blogstorm**, but in the form of a race.

blowback *noun*
1. unintended adverse results arising from an action or a situation. 2. the inevitable consequences of a foolish business decision, generally dealt with by other parties after the person responsible for the decision has safely left the scene of the crime.

blow-by-blow description *adjective*
in bruising detail, one thumping, excruciating mental image after another.

blue-chip *adjective*
1. of a well respected company with a large business core, and global reach. 2. beyond the reach of the law, in cahoots with government and third-world dictatorships. 3. considerably more important than you; not to be messed with.

blue-sky thinking *noun*
1. **out-of-the-box** thinking, unfettered by rationality, unconstrained by real-world, real-time considerations; "what if" **brainstorming**. 2. bullshit.

bottom line *noun*
1. profit; what it's all about. 2. when all's said and done, and made and sold, **at the end of the day**, the money that's been raked in.

brainchild *noun*
1. product of one's thought; an invention; an original idea. 2. another attempt at claiming to be godlike in having the ability to create things.

brain dump *noun*
providing all of the information, typically when someone is handing over an initiative, or, condescendingly, grooming a successor.

brainfart *noun*
1. the by-product of a bloated mind expressing thoughts and opinions randomly and witlessly. 2. a burst of possibly useful information produced by accident.

brainstorm *verb*
1. attempt to reach imaginatively beyond obvious solutions. 2. to come up with obviously ludicrous suggestions in an attempt to get the boss off your back (be warned, though, that this may result in your ludicrous suggestions being adopted and you being put in charge of implementing them).

brainstorming *noun*
a business buzzword for the collective cogitations of brains unleashed in concert to mount an attack on a problem from every possible point of view (its use was once banned in British Broadcasting Corporation internal memos for being offensive to epileptics).

brand *noun*
1. **product** manufactured by a company and given a specific name or mark; a trademark; a kind, type, or variety. 2. a mark of disgrace; a hot iron used for branding. 3. **brand** *verb* to mark by burning. 4. to attempt, in a transparently bogus fashion, to differentiate a bland, generic **product** from its pack of competitors.

bread and butter *noun*
1. maintenance; livelihood; source of income. 2. **bread-and-butter** *adjective* habitual, routine, usual, practical, material – in short, something that is *deeply* boring.

bricks-and-clicks *adjective*
1. a business model by which a company integrates both its offline (**bricks**) and online (**clicks**) presence. 2. an attempt at world domination by a company in which it saturates all possible sales areas (also sometimes

referred to as **bricks-clicks-and-flips**, "flips" being catalogs).

bubble thinking *noun*
1. a business strategy based on the assumption that "bubble conditions" (e.g. a mania in which prices are bid up by **bulls**) will last indefinitely. 2. a cause of bankruptcy, at which point the exponents of **bubble thinking** will point out that no one could possibly have predicted that the market for tulips/South Sea shares/dotcom start-ups/condos in Kazakhstan would ever crash.

budget *noun*
a projection of income and expenditure for the upcoming year (or other period), usually fatally flawed by overestimating sales and underestimating costs.

budget meeting *noun*
an excruciating discussion of exactly why sales figures have been overestimated and expenditure underestimated, resulting in a new **budget** for the following year which makes even more extravagant claims and promises in an attempt to protect the position of the employee responsible.

bull *cf.* **bear** *noun*
a deranged optimist who believes that prices always go up and who gambles accordingly (a **bull** often makes large **paper fortunes** before pathetically squandering them on the latest speculative bubble).

bull trap *noun*
a brief spike in prices before the real crash begins.

business cycle *noun*
1. a ready-made, multipurpose excuse for terrible sales figures. 2. the process of swings and roundabouts whereby everything is turned on its head: this year's profit becomes next year's loss; this year's Employee of the Year becomes next year's whipping boy; and so on.

business lunch *noun*
an overpriced meal, eaten with colleagues or **customers** (for some reason, people eating **business lunches** generally behave boorishly and drink too much, perhaps the hysteria caused by a few moments out of the office, or perhaps just by the fact that it really is a free lunch).

business-macho *adjective*
descriptive of a male office worker with his shirt opened too far at the neck – at least one button beyond what could be considered business casual (often accented by tufts of chest hair and/or gold chains).

business model *noun*
1. the modus operandi of a business; how it actually operates. 2. a polite way of saying "whatever it takes to make a buck."

business needs *noun*
1. a business *desires* profits – to make profits it requires its **needs** to be met: raw materials, credit, manpower, machinery, and so on. 2. the basic requirements for running a successful business. 3. the degree to which one's basic humanity needs to be subsumed in and crushed by the corporate environment.

business plan *noun*
a fantasy put forward in an attempt to hoodwink one's bank manager or a venture capitalist into signing a large, essentially blank, cheque.

business process re-engineering *noun*
firing people.

business-provocative *adjective*
work attire that is sexy to the point of being inappropriate ("I see Kim has decided that the dress code for today is **business-provocative**.").

businessspeak, also **businessese**, **corporatese** *noun*
1. incoherent, unintelligible gibberish. 2. an arcane language, intelligible only to initiates, which describes inviolable truths at the heart of the world of commerce.

buy one, get one free
an offer that makes it painfully obvious how much profit the manufacturer makes on the normal price.

buzz *noun*
excitement surrounding a new **product**, sometimes even preceding its launch, like bees around flowers (or flies around shit).

buzzword *noun*
a voguish word, often recently made up, which is widely used, but the exact meaning of which remains unclear, or ambivalent, largely deliberately, as the use of buzzwords is intended to impress rather than enlighten. For example, the following sentence while liberally dotted with **buzzwords** (in bold) – "We need to create a **dynamic**

framework to **facilitate empowerment**" – has very little, if any, actual meaning.

buzzword-compliant *adjective*
of a **product** which supports features, or of a CV or exam answer which uses words that are currently highly fashionable, as in, "I'm not sure that it actually works properly, but it's **buzzword-compliant** and that's the main thing."

C

call into question *verb*
1. to cast doubt on. 2. to gently query something. 3. to undermine the entire basis of a course of action, or a conclusion.
4. the kiss of death for an idea, someone's career, etc.

cannibalization *noun*
1. the act of removing parts from one thing, such as an object or machine, to be used in another. 2. a vicious action resulting in loss of sales of an existing **product** to a new **product** offered by another company. 3. a megalomaniac stealing someone else's ideas and getting credit and being rewarded for them.

cannibalize *verb*
1. to adapt and re-use past ideas or **products**. 2. to come as close to copyright theft as possible while remaining just the right side of the law.

Can we have a talk?
a warning sign that your boss is about to explain in excruciating detail how disappointed he or she is by your performance.

career drift *cf.* **lateralled**
a sideways move, without promotion, in a stagnating career; usually sold as "career development," but, in fact, **flatlining**.

celebrate *verb*
1. to observe (a day) or commemorate (an event) with ceremonies or festivities. 2. to make known publicly; to proclaim. 3. to spend time with colleagues in a spirit of enforced joviality. 4. to recognize the pitifully minor achievement of a lowly employee, that he or she has, for example, sold more of whatever **product** the company happens to sell than anyone else in the branch that week.

change is good
chances are you're about to be "let go of" due to "**challenging** economic conditions," though the irritation may be more minor, such as being moved to a desk out in the passage, or on another floor – or outside, where the smokers go.

challenging *adjective*
1. difficult, placing extra demands on people, as in "running a business in a **challenging** economic environment." 2. frankly impossible, as in "being given a **challenging** assignment" – there is no way in which anyone could successfully complete the task that you've been given, so don't even try.

channels *noun*
1. the correct ways within a business or organization to direct complaints, requests, and so on. 2. the means for getting your own way, by whatever it takes.

chartist *noun*
an economist who relies on charts of past business cycles to predict the future – you might be better off asking an astrologer.

checked out
of someone who is no longer fully engaged in a project, for example, when he or she is giving notice; present in body, but not in mind – mentally, he or she has already **checked out**.

clicks-and-mortar *adjective*
cynical and desperate money-grubbing. See **bricks-and-clicks**.

client-focused *adjective*
identifying and responding to current and future client needs, the better to swindle them.

close, but no cigar
to come disappointingly close to success – just not quite good enough for any reward.

coachable *adjective*
1. when one has one's habits, hang-ups, assumptions, and lack of self-confidence under control, one is said to be **coachable**, or, in other words, receptive to new knowledge and new ways of doing things. 2. a **coachable** employee is a clean slate on which a business may make its mark,

unimpeded. 3. willing to abandon personal ethics and friendships in pursuit of money and/or power.

collaborative *adjective*
1. descriptive of working together with others on a particular project – this requires trust on your part, if you are interested in the outcome, or it can offer a way of getting out of doing too much work if you are not interested in the end result. 2. descriptive of work being meddled with needlessly and unjustifiably by **colleagues**. 3. descriptive of work botched jointly by a group of **colleagues**, rather than by one individual.

colleague *noun*
1. someone with whom you work. 2. a word sinisterly stripped of any previous, positive associations to do with friendship or comradely mutual endeavour; a competitor in the office rat race, someone ever-ready to stab you in the back, or whisper behind it.

commitment *noun*
1. engagement; involvement. 2. a pledge or promise; an obligation. 3. a condition of employment, that an employee should display this level of devotion to whatever the task may be, nothing less than the level of commitment expected of a couple getting married, or the self-abnegating fervour of a young monk inducted into a religious cult.

communicate that to *verb*
1. tell. 2. do someone's dirty work for them, especially if the likely response will be hostility and/or anger.

community *noun*
1. a group of people living together in one place, especially one practising common ownership of resources. 2. cynical advertising-speak for lumping people together in a group for marketing purposes in order to sell them tat, in line with their perceived level of stupidity.

comparative pricing *noun*
an attempt to undercut competitors by the bare minimum necessary.

compelling *adjective*
1. convincing, persuasive; binding, constraining; urgent, pressing. 2. can also refer to a belief system where all the evidence appears to be stacked up against you, in which case it's probably best to hide.

competitive advantage *noun*
1. some slight advantage over a competitor, enabling a company to pull ahead. 2. an overweening, crushing advantage, like the ability of an enormous chain of stores to buy goods in bulk, pile them high, and sell them cheap, thereby squeezing out small and disunited competitors.

consensus *noun*
1. a majority of opinion. 2. the bare minimum of consent required from a claque of yes-men before some decision is railroaded through. 3. a failure to ask anyone, in case someone disagrees.

conservatively *adverb*
1. cautiously. 2. a weasel-word used to modify various estimates, to suggest that much more is to be hoped for: "**Conservatively**, we estimate that we will break even

within the next two months." ("We expect to be rolling in cash, shortly.") 3. a modifier used to acknowledge, coyly, that the writer doesn't really have a clue: "Bill Gates's fortune is **conservatively** estimated at $56 billion."

content *noun*
1. the information contained in any particular format, e.g. website **content**, TV program **content**, newspaper **content**. 2. smugly happy or satisfied.

content management system *noun*
1. a pretentious word for a text editor 2. a computer application which creates more work than it saves.

convergence *noun*
1. a way of assembly, of coming together. 2. people showing a tendency to evolve superficially similar characteristics under similar environmental conditions, such as in the workplace or when shopping. 3. the lumping together of many bad **products** or practices in the hope of making them more appealing.

core business *noun*
1. an idealized construct intended to express an organization's "main" or "essential" activity (in reality, this is often coffee-making, bitching, and procrastinating). 2. the only aspect of a business in which its employees are even vaguely proficient.

core competency *noun*
1. something which a company or an individual can do well, which provides benefits to **customers**, is difficult for competitors to imitate, and which can be applied to many different **products** and markets. 2. when the tinsel is

stripped away, the only thing that a company or individual can be relied on to do half-way competently.

core technology *noun*
1. in computer-speak, a **core** refers to a processor, its cache and cache controller; a dual core would link within one CPU (Central Processing Unit) two such **cores**, while a multi-core CPU would combine more than two. 2. having seeped out of the world of computers and into the language of the MBA, **core technology** refers to that technology without which a manager would be lost, i.e. mobile phone and **BlackBerry**.

corporate bullshit *noun*
a language which looks and sounds like English, but is, in reality, composed solely of half-truths, lies, and propaganda spewed forth by big corporations in the hope of turning people into obedient consumers and getting them to part with their hard-earned cash.

corporate responsibility *noun*
see **corporation**.

corporate streamlining
1. job cuts. 2. people being fired.

corporation *noun*
legal entity designed to avoid any possibility of **corporate responsibility**.

CrackBerry *cf.* **BlackBerry** *noun*
1. a **BlackBerry**, "a wireless **e-mail** solution for mobile professionals." Philippe Reines, a thirty-something Democrat employed on Capitol Hill, described developing

CrackBerry withdrawal on Martha's Vineyard, where he wandered around for days hoping to find reception, before pleading with an airline employee to take his **BlackBerry** on a round trip to where it could send and receive messages. In the course of the round trip, his **BlackBerry** received 129 new messages.

creative team noun
1. the creators of content for a project. 2. workers soon to be replaced by computers and focus groups. 3. prima donnas, usually found outside smoking, perhaps drinking espresso, and bitching about their colleagues.

criteria, a *noun*
1. the plural of criterion used, incorrectly, in the singular. 2. principle or standard by which something may be judged or decided, especially when one needs to be hyper-critical during an appraisal.

critical path *noun*
the appropriate steps to be taken in a crisis (before anyone finds out what you've done).

cross-functional *adjective*
1. a **cross-functional** team is a group of people with different areas of expertise working together towards a common goal – not to be confused with "dysfunctional" or working at "cross purposes." 2. a team unable to function adequately in *any* area of expertise, and unlikely to achieve any goal.

cross-media *adjective*
media which invites the viewer or listener to cross from one medium to another, for example, from radio to the internet – not to be confused with "crossed wires."

cross-platform *adjective*
1. a term that describes a language, software application or hardware device that works on more than one system. 2. descriptive of someone who can operate in many different environments, and who is often used and abused for this.

cultivate *verb*
1. to grow or create. 2. to sort and assess any amount of recently obtained marijuana prior to smoking it. 3. to prepare the ground for planting new ideas, especially in people, pretending to develop, improve or nurture them in return for them doing things your way.

curve breaker *noun*
1. a compliment bestowed on someone who has devised a genuinely new way of working, the curve being the pattern of normal distribution. 2. a real smarty-pants.

customer *noun*
1. pleb, idiot. 2. source of money. 3. important and valued element of a company's **business model** (*archaic*).

customer-centric *adjective*
probably not, but that's the idea, isn't it? Of course the business is "centred" on **customers**; there wouldn't be one otherwise, would there?

customer service *noun*
1. a company's willingness to do what the **customer** wants rather than what the company wants (*archaic*). 2. platitudes enshrined in a document which is seldom consulted. 3. the use of computers to obfuscate the sales process and otherwise frustrate **customers**.

customer service orientation *noun*
1. a willingness to pander to customers' every need and desire. 2. the inability of an employee to recognize that the company is more important than its customers, usually culminating in dismissal.

customized *adjective*
a process or **product** adapted using someone else's idea.

cutting-edge *adjective*
1. not quite **bleeding-edge**, but not far off, either – companies rely on **cutting-edge** technology to give them a **competitive advantage** in pursuing the **Big Win**. 2. **cutting edge** *noun* e.g. "This system is hugely expensive because it is at the **cutting edge** of design."

cut to the chase
get to the point, quickly, by leaving aside the crushingly dull accumulation of facts and figures in a presentation – an expression from the early days of film-making when directors were advised to leap forward from their ploddingly dull story lines to a chase scene of some kind, involving horses, or, more recently, cars. An expression usually barked at employees by "time-poor" bosses.

CV

1. a summary of basic facts about a prospective employee.
2. farrago of lies intended to persuade an employer to pay an incompetent sociopath to pretend to do his or her job.

cyclical bull move in a secular bear market, a

1. a secular market refers to a much longer time frame (eight to twenty years) when the general movement in the value of stocks is in one direction (**bear** = down; **bull** = up). Cyclical movements, taking place over a much shorter time frame, continue to occur within secular markets, sometimes in opposition to the prevailing trend. 2. a riddle wrapped in a mystery inside an enigma. 3. the pundits have no idea what is going on.

D

delayer *verb*
See **delayering**.

delayering *noun*
1. flattening the managerial hierarchy. 2. cutting out the middle managers. 3. firing people.

deliver *verb*
1. to convey – a parcel, for example. 2. to bring about: "to **deliver** continuous improvement within an organization." 3. quite simply, to "do".

deliverables *noun*
1. goods or services that can be exchanged – for money, usually. 2. something that can be delivered, from "increased productivity" to "**customer** satisfaction." 3. your efficiency at work is measured according to the extent to which you **deliver** on what have been determined to be your **deliverables** – still with us?

demographic *noun*
1. **demographics** is the study of the structure of human populations using statistics relating to births, deaths, wealth, disease, etc. 2. A **demographic** is a category used by advertisers and marketers to corral individuals into a more manageable herd of obedient consumers to whom they can dictate various spurious "needs" and "desires."

deploy *verb*
yet another macho borrowing from military terminology; just as a general deploys troops and weaponry on the battlefield, a CEO **deploys** his workers and resources to seize strategic objectives in the marketplace.

dictates *noun*
the **dictates** of the marketplace, for example, are the immutable laws laid down by the all-powerful market, before which we are all mere minions, enslaved, **dictated** to.

difference, what a . . . a year/month/day makes
very little, invariably.

differential *noun*
1. the difference allowed by a futures contract with regard to the quality of what will be delivered and where it will be delivered to (also known as an "allowance") 2. often used as a pompous (and incorrect) stand-in for "difference" in corporate documents, e.g. "We need to plan for the **differential** between what we have promised and what we are, in fact, able to deliver."

different this time, it's
oh no, it's not.

disintermediate *verb*
1. to reduce the use of banks and savings institutions as intermediaries in the borrowing and investment of money, in favour of direct involvement in the securities market such as the diversion of savings from accounts with low fixed interest rates to direct investment in high-yielding but unstable investments. 2. to eliminate an intermediary in a transaction between two parties, invariably in order to save money, and invariably shafting someone in the process. 3. to shaft.

disseminate *verb*
1. to scatter or spread widely, as though sowing seed; promulgate extensively; broadcast. 2. to spread the word, to ensure that no **colleague** is left **out of the loop**. 3. to sow the wild oats of your achievements far and wide in the hope that little seeds of admiration will take root among your colleagues.

diversity *noun*
1. the holy grail of the politically correct workplace, the creation of a modern-day Tower of Babel, a high-rise clamour of mutual unintelligibility. 2. tokenism: the positioning of a handful of workers representing favoured minority groups a little bit closer to the ground-floor windows.

dog days *noun pl.*
1. a period when it is clear that someone is going to be fired, but it is not yet clear who. 2. a prolonged period of depressed mood in an office during which not much business at all is transacted.

domain expertise *noun*
specialist skills and knowledge possessed by a **domain expert** (also known as a Subject Matter Expert, or SME), as in, "We need an SME now with the required **domain expertise** to get on top of this issue about which we understand next to nothing."

dot-com *noun*
1. an abbreviation for a company which conducts its business primarily on the internet. 2. an overhyped internet-related company, seemingly above and beyond any conventional rules of business, which produces nothing, but burns investors' money almost as quickly as they can keep shovelling it in, as occurred during the orgy of greed and lack of restraint which was the "**dot-com** bubble."

dotted-line relationship *noun*
a situation in which a person has dual responsibilities, for example, to a line manager as well as to a project team; the mainstay of **matrix** organizations (the temptation exists to "cut along the dotted line" when priorities conflict).

download *verb*
1. to take on board the information relating to a specific situation. 2. to allow malware and spyware to mess up your computer.

downsize *verb*
to fire people.

downsizing *noun*
1. getting smaller, shrinking. 2. firing people, then firing some more (can be continued ad infinitum till the boss is

left all alone on the top floor wondering why no one responds to his or her **e-mails**).

drill down *verb*
1. to bore down into the ground in the hope of coming across oil or precious gemstones (or something). 2. to break a problem down into its component parts, and keep doing so until you have a grasp of everything that is contributing to the problem that you are facing; at this stage you will have a thoroughly dismantled problem, though probably one that is no less intractable.

drive *noun*
1. to have drive is to be annoyingly pushy, particularly in pursuit of a goal 2. a quality much admired by bosses in looking to appoint underlings to do their bidding, zealously.

ducks in a row, to have one's
1. to be organized; to be on top of things. 2. an expression beloved of MBA graduates, derived from the kitsch practice of having three flying ducks nailed to the living room wall (people claiming to have their **ducks in a row** are, in fact, often indulging in something uncannily similar to the interior decor precedent; their appearance of being precisely ordered and enjoying high-flying success is a sham, merely decorative – their "ducks" are no more real than those nailed to the living room wall).

due diligence *noun*
1. a flimsy, flawed investigation of the finances of a company targeted for acquisition. 2. the failure to spot blindingly obvious contractual, legal, and accounting nightmares prior to a takeover.

dynamic *adjective*
like a dynamo, fizzing and sparking with energy and ideas; **dynamic** people are much admired in the business world as they are full of go and the **drive** to implement their crackpot schemes. Whether these ever go anywhere or achieve anything is beside the point; dynamic people create an air of busyness, indispensable in any office environment.

dynamic analysis *noun*
1. the analysis of the properties of a running program. 2. updating your analysis in real time, as a situation unfolds . . . **hitting the ground running** . . . keeping your wits about you . . . moving fast in a fast-moving environment, and so on and on. 3. an intentionally vacuous phrase, used by management consultants to make doing nothing sound like a big deal.

E

e-business, **e-commerce** *noun*
1. a cheap way of doing business electronically without needing to pay real, live employees to speak to **customers** and without having to pay to rent or buy retail premises. 2. a popular way of **outsourcing** work to the kind of countries where workers can be paid as little as a dollar a day to deal with irate **customers** at the end of their tether.

e-enable *verb*
1. to make 85 per cent of a workforce redundant and hire cheap labour overseas by relocating your company from the real world to cyberspace. 2. to facilitate something, with a slight stutter.

elephant in the room, the
a major problem or controversial issue which is quite obviously present, but is avoided as a subject for discussion because it is more comfortable to pretend that there is no elephant.

e-mail *noun/verb*
communication technology that allows people to avoid talking to each other.

e-markets *noun pl.*
1. the global financial markets at the push of a button. 2. a way for bankers and other rich bastards to benefit from easy, secure trading, real-time market information from around the world, and ready access to analytical tools – to get richer, in other words, with even greater ease.

embedded skills set *noun*
1. the ability to do something, having had it drummed in by rote learning. 2. in a word, skills.

embrace *verb*
1. to hug, to hold tight, to wrap one's arms around someone or something; to accept, include, surround, and possibly suffocate. 2. to finally succumb to corporate groupthink and adopt wholesale the firm's ways of doing things, with scarcely credible fervour.

employee phase-out *noun*
firing people, slowly.

employee satisfaction *noun*
ha ha ha.

empower *verb*
1. to give authority or power to, to authorize, to give strength and confidence to. 2. to give employees the power to take on challenges which are likely to destroy them, as surely as a boulder dislodged on a mountainside. 3. to give people enough rope with which to hang

themselves. 4. often used reflexively by hairy-legged women as an excuse for making themselves wilfully ugly.

endangered species *noun*
a category of worker threatened by impending legislation, e.g. local call centre workers.

end-to-end *adjective*
1. attribute of a protocol that functions on the origin and the final destination but not on any intermediate stages. 2. (in **e-commerce**) describes a connection between people wanting to sell and people wanting to buy, a practice which eliminates middlemen, i.e. employees, who merely extract value from the trade by requiring to be paid, thereby increasing profits.

engage *verb*
1. to keep busy, occupy; employ; attract; commit and bind (to fulfill an obligation). 2. another military borrowing, as in "to **engage** with the enemy": to "take on" competitors. 3. to **engage** with **customers**/clients/suppliers: to listen to them, and tell them how you **envisage** their role in your success.

engineer *verb*
to make, in a word (problems are no longer simply solved – **solutions** are **engineered**).

enhance *verb*
1. to improve the quality, value, or extent of something, sometimes off a very low base indeed. 2. to give a deceptive gloss to tat, e.g. to polish a turd.

enterprise-wide *adjective*
right across a business (in other words, absolutely everyone will be subjected to the new diktat emanating from the head office). Example: "We will be rolling this out **enterprise-wide 24/7**."

envision *verb*
1. an exciting, new, made-up word to take the place of the pre-existing **envisage**, which had, for many years, successfully meant exactly the same thing: to imagine, conceive. 2. to see yourself as a shimmering, god-like success in an idealized future.

envisioneer *verb*
1. to **envision** (not happy with their previous, needless invention, those tireless corporate generators of bullshit had to beef it up with the addition of -eer). 2. a portmanteau word combining elements of **engineer** with **envision** – to construct the future in your mind, preparatory to inflicting it on the world.

equity *noun*
the overestimated value of your assets minus the underestimated value of your liabilities (if your assets were honestly worth that much, why wouldn't you simply sell up and move to the Bahamas?).

equivalents *noun pl.*
things that are equivalent, equal in value, except that, usually, they are not – they have merely been decreed to be equivalent, to the advantage of one party in a transaction.

e-services *noun*
1. a generic term usually referring to the provision of services via the internet; webspeak for just about anything done on the internet (can cause confusion when used in conjunction with "support," because nobody knows the difference between **e-services** and online support). 2. **e-services** incorporate **e-commerce**, and they may also include non-commercial services such as government **e-services**, though we may need to begin to define "services."

e-solution *noun*
a solution to your **e-problem**, which you might not have been aware that you had (a prime example of the internet's "give us your money and don't ask so many questions" approach). An **e-solution** is something to do with doing business on the internet, but no one is exactly sure what – perhaps it makes your website more attractive, or more visible, but it's a must-have and you have to pay for it.

e-tailer *noun*
1. an online retailer without a physical address, stock, staff, a telephone number, social skills, etc. 2. a cutesy reworking of "retailer" in time-honoured e-fashion.

etched in stone
something that could be said to be fairly definite, i.e. not "pencilled in," or prescriptive – a rule to be obeyed without fail, for example, "The deadline for the completion of the report is **etched in stone**; there will be no extension," or, "The procedure to be followed in such circumstances is **etched in stone**. Deviate from it, even slightly, at the risk of losing your job."

evasion strategy
see **wild goose chase**.

evolving *adjective*
developing, gradually changing, unfolding, for example,
"This is an evolving situation," i.e., "We don't really
know what's going on," or, "We see your role in the
company as an evolving one," i.e., "We're going to keep
piling on responsibilities, depending on how much you
seem able to take."

excremental *cf.* **incremental** *adjective*
shitty, e.g., "As opposed to experiencing an **incremental**,
or gradual, increase in sales, our sales figures for the year
have been **excremental** to say the least."

exemplary *adjective*
1. setting an example; being so good or admirable that
others would do well to copy you, but will instead
probably accuse you of brown-nosing behind your back.
2. serving as an example, e.g. "You have disappointed me
and I intend your punishment to be **exemplary** in order to
deter others."

existing standards
the status quo, the way things are (the use of this term is
usually an indication that the situation is about to be
changed dramatically, that current substandard behaviours
and processes are about to be radically overhauled).

expedite *verb*
to make things quicker; to facilitate, e.g. "I will **expedite**
the writing of the report," in other words, "I will write the
report more quickly," or, more ominously, "I will *have* the

report written more quickly," meaning that someone is about to have a fire lit under them – **expedite** is used under the (mistaken) impression that it sounds more active and aggressive than simply speeding something up, or doing it more quickly.

exploit *verb*
1. to selfishly use or take advantage of another person with little or no regard for their desires or pleasures. 2. to manipulate to the greatest possible personal advantage, as in "**exploiting** one's skills or talents." 3. **exploit** *noun* a bold or daring feat often involving a practical joke, or the humiliation of somebody in some fashion.

extend *verb*
1. to make larger or longer in space or time. 2. to hold something out towards someone – either a peace offering, or a punishment. 3. to push someone to the limits of their endurance, e.g. "This new role in the company will extend your capabilities." 4. to prolong the "useful" life of some essentially useless piece of equipment by superficial tinkering, e.g. "We can **extend** the life of your pump by replacing the seal on this valve – here is our bill."

extensible *adjective*
1. *computer science* of a program, language, or protocol that can be expanded by having its capabilities added to. 2. of a program, language, or protocol which is rushed into the marketplace, far from complete, still requiring much **extension** for it to be of any use at all.

eyeball *verb*
1. another noun pressed into service in **businessspeak** as a verb, meaning to stare at closely, in a hostile manner (to

face up to someone "**eyeball** to **eyeball**" is to stand your ground in a hostile fashion). 2. to examine someone or something intently with a view to making a critical evaluation, or a choice.

F

facilitate *verb*
to make easier, or less difficult, to make possible, to smooth the way for, to oil the wheels of, to **expedite**, e.g., "Following recent job losses you will be provided with training and resources to **facilitate** your re-entry into the job market."

fact-based management *noun*
1. using the facts derived from evaluating and assessing a business process to restructure the process in order to **maximize** profits. 2. the opposite of **blue-sky**, or pie-in-the-sky, management, when anything goes, and management is under no obligation to tether itself to dull reality.

fad surfing *noun*
the process whereby managers leap on each passing bandwagon of change to strut their stuff, turning offices and processes upside down, before leaping onto the next wagon which happens to trundle past.

fallback position *noun*
1. a safe refuge, yet another macho military borrowing. If the assault by the sales force on the commanding heights of the industry, currently held by the company's opponents, fails, the bugle can be blown and the wearied workers can retreat to the **fallback position** of clinging grimly to the company's existing market share. 2. *negotiation* if an aggressive negotiating gambit has failed, the negotiator can slink back to the **fallback position** of what his or her opponent has already conceded.

falling on his/her/your sword *verb*
the honourable thing for a boss to do if he or she has screwed up, often suggested in a clamour by media commentators. No half measures here; simply to resign just wouldn't cut the mustard, though the imagery does at least stop short of *hara kiri*, or ritual disembowelment. Also: **fall on his/her/your truncheon/pen/etc**. for use with police officers, writers, etc.

fast-track *verb*
1. to prioritize, implement speedily (a gung-ho, highly active verb), e.g. "I'd like you to **fast-track** the implementation of this project, so that we can have it up and running as quickly as possible." 2. to promote an employee rapidly beyond his or her level of ability.

feedback *noun*
1. the screeching sound produced by a microphone being placed too close to a speaker. 2. unsolicited opinions on how you are doing in the workplace. 3. harsh criticism, usually unsought, and unwanted. And unhelpful.

first-mover advantage *noun*
1. the advantage gained by the initial occupant of a market segment; the company or individual which makes the first move is able to gain control of resources before competitors. 2. a smug riff on "the early bird gets the worm."

flag *verb*
1. to mark for future attention. An issue arising in a meeting, rather than being dealt with, may be **flagged** for further investigation or to be dealt with at a subsequent meeting. 2. to brush past a problem in the hope that it will simply disappear before any action needs to be taken.

flatlining *cf.* **career drift**, **lateralled**
1. a "career" which is drifting sideways, without promotion. 2. dead, in a clinical sense.

focus group *noun*
1. a group of people brought together as part of a research strategy in which researchers attempt to discover the opinions of the public regarding **products**. 2. a group of people brought together in an attempt to manufacture supporting evidence for the commissioning of a flimsy or otherwise worthless **product**.

follow-up *noun*
1. the maintainence of contact so as to monitor the effects of earlier activities or treatments. 2. continuing harassment by an employer or telephone call centre constantly demanding answers to pointless questions.

frictionless *adjective*
1. of the goal of simplifying employee access to a company's IT resources; in reality, most often a source of profound friction, sometimes leading to spontaneous combustion. 2. of a transaction, a takeover, or a dismissal: problem-free, smooth.

from an historical point of view
an expression used to preface an absurdly positive view of something, often presented during a sales meeting; the **historical point of view** is often entirely unreconcilable with with historical fact.

front-end *verb*
to prioritize, in a word – jargon as ugly, and needless, as its synonym, e.g. "I'd like you to **front-end** work on the high-priority accounts" which sounds alarmingly like taking a bulldozer to them.

front lines *noun*
1. any area of potential or actual conflict or struggle. 2. *business* more borrowed military jargon, a term used to describe employees, often in service industries, who have to deal directly with **customers**, in which role they are usually allowed only to reiterate company policy, and are disallowed from responding logically to **customer** queries and complaints.

full-time *adjective*
1. of working or operating the entire time, considered standard or customary for a specific activity; involving or taking up the whole of the time available. 2. of the devotion of a person's full energies to work, leaving little or no energy for dealing with friends, family and other distractions.

functionality *noun*
1. functional capability; the way something works or operates, or online, what purpose it serves, e.g., a website which allows people to purchase an item online has a **functionality** which is distinct from one that simply lets users post and read other people's information or shows only a catalog of **products**. 2. the supposed opposite of dysfunctionality, but all too often too close to it for comfort.

fusion *noun*
1. the binding of two or more things, tangible or intangible, into something new that possesses properties of both, but often the quality of neither. 2. A melting, smelting; blend, mixture, combination; union; coalescence; paste. 3. a mess, chaos. 4. an unappealing mix of two incompatible substances.

Bullshit Job Titles

Generate your own bullshit job title, or help someone else with theirs. Simply combine one word, chosen randomly, from each column to generate a new title.

Lead	Solutions	Supervisor
Senior	Program	Associate
Direct	Brand	Executive
Corporate	Security	Liaison
Dynamic	Research	Officer
Future	Marketing	Manager
Product	Directives	Engineer
National	Implementation	Specialist
Regional	Integration	Director
District	Functionality	Co-ordinator

G

game plan *noun*
1. a lot of business bullshit comes from the world of sport, particularly baseball and American football – a **game plan** is an overall strategy (as has been said of **battle plans**, a **game plan** is unlikely to survive contact with competitors).

gap analysis *noun*
1. a business resource assessment tool enabling a company to compare its actual performance with its potential. 2. a management strategy to try to figure out how useful the staff are.

generate *verb*
to cause to arise or to come about; both chaos and wealth can be generated, as can heat, and light, e.g., "The implementation of the new management strategy **generated** almost instantaneous chaos."

get off on the wrong foot *verb*
1. to launch off on the wrong foot in attempting to surmount some obstacle, like a hurdle, usually resulting in clipping the obstacle with one foot or the other and ending up sprawled on the ground. 2. to make a bad start in a job or relationship, with largely similar consequences.

get on the same page *verb cf.* **on the same page**
to move from points of mutual incomprehension or virtual irreconcilability to roughly the same position; to prepare to tackle a problem with someone else from roughly the same starting point, as opposed to from a page in a different book, in a different library.

get things off your chest *verb*
to have a good moan or bitch about someone, to a third party, to be able to relax and move on in the same way that one might after freeing oneself from under a heavy log or other deadweight. Be wary of an invitation from the boss **to get things off your chest**, though, as this is most likely an attempt to draw you out and into a trap; getting things off one's chest is best done out of the workplace and among close friends.

globalization *noun*
1. adaptation of the world economy to a state of permanent interaction. 2. a state in which costs and wages in every country in the world fall to the lowest common denominator. 3. the preferred state of multinational corporations. 4. empire; freedom; slavery; exploitation – pick your favourite interpretation.

global player *noun*
usually descriptive of a small company with unlikely ambitions (beware the boss who continuously reiterates a desire to build a company into a **global player** – employees are likely to be worked to death in pursuit of a chimera).

going forward *cf.* **at this moment in time** *archaic*
a meaningless "tag", the equivalent of the now outmoded **at this moment in time**. Compare "We are selling 20,000 jube-jubes a month **going forward/at this moment in time**" with "We are selling 20,000 jube-jubes a month."

go-to-market strategy *noun*
a plan for selling newly developed, unwanted tat to unwilling consumers.

granular *adjective*
characterized by a high level of complicated detail in a set of data, e.g. "Can we make this **granular**?" (a request for more detail), or "This information is too **granular**" when you can't understand it or someone assumes that you are of below average intelligence.

grow *verb*
1. to develop or expand an enterprise or business; to become larger or greater over time. 2. a request to germinate and develop ideas. 3. to attempt to satisfy stockholders' insatiable demands for higher dividends, using inherently risky investment strategies.

guesstimate *noun*
1. a half-assed estimate. 2. A supposedly educated guess or aproximation, but, in reality, an annoying word probably dreamed up by high school science teachers, which means neither "guess" nor "estimate."

H

hands-on *adjective*
1. of an intimate relationship between a manager and an underling, or a worker and a task; a **hands-on** manager is one who is fond of meddling in, or micro-managing, his employees' work.

hardball *noun*
"to play **hardball**" in negotiations is to be unwilling to compromise, to be inflexible and ruthless. This is a favourite negotiation strategy of corporate bosses not given to nuance or subtlety. Sometimes it serves to bully opponents into submission; usually, though, the result is deadlock as two opponents play **hardball** with each other to no one's benefit.

harness *verb*
1. to control, rein in or utilize an idea or resources, as in "to **harness** the power of nature," or "to harness the energy and creativity of employees." 2. can also be used as a polite term for stealing someone else's ideas.

have a conversation, to *verb*
1. on the face of it, "**to have a conversation**" is to talk with someone, but, in reality, the kiss of death if suggested by one's boss, as in, "Could you come up, please, I'd like **to have a conversation**." The ensuing conversation may well end in your being fired, or a dressing down or reprimand of some kind, possibly involving humiliation. 2. to look for ways to disregard someone's input, as in "**have a conversation** with the **customer**/supplier/creative team."

heads-up *noun*
an advance warning, usually of an impending catastrophe heading your way; a detailed description of the piece of shit which is flying towards the fan, the speed at which the fan is rotating, your position in relationship to the fan, and the likely splatter pattern.

heads will roll
1. people will be fired. Another military borrowing from a time less "soft" than our own, when failure meant execution, usually by being beheaded. The image of a guillotine dispensing justice is conjured up for people being forced to resign. 2. a scapegoat will be found.

hedge fund *noun*
a secretive financial body that claims to be able to make massive profits. Its basic strategy is claimed to be "hedging" whereby huge amounts are gambled both on stocks going up and, in case this goes wrong, on stocks moving in the opposite direction. As any gambler knows, there is no such winning system in life. In fact **hedge funds**' apparently magical profits are generated by taking jaw-dropping risks with **leverage**, which is one reason why many of them disappear in a puff of smoke in a stock market slump.

high-impact *adjective*

a marketing strategy focused on the effect which it is likely to have on its target audience – shock tactics and emotional blackmail are popular **high-impact** techniques.

hiring freeze *noun*

the cold blast of disappointment which confronts unwanted job-seekers who find their hopes dashed by a company's decision to stop hiring – apart from the other people interviewed on the same day as you (a very localized **hiring freeze**).

hitting the ground running

1. leaping from the back of a moving truck, rifle at the ready, prepared to take on whatever is about to be thrown at you. 2. finding yourself in a fast-paced and physically overwhelming situation, the sensation heightened by a sense of confusion and personal ineptness, more like simply hitting the ground (no running involved).

holistic *adjective*

1. an unusual appearance of terminology from complementary therapies in the world of business, **holistic** suggests that each and every aspect of an enterprise, for example, is being nurtured. 2. a favoured adjective of ex-hippies who have belatedly discovered their inner capitalist.

Homer, to pull a

to succeed in spite of being a complete idiot, derived from the exploits of animated TV star Homer Simpson.

horizontal merger *noun*

1. a merger in which two companies offering similar services pool their resources and improve their service to

the **customer** (*archaic*). 2. an aggressive buy-out, an attempt to eliminate a competitor. 3. an asset-stripping operation. 4. an attempt to turn an oligopoly into a monopoly.

hot item *noun*
1. something which is in great demand, usually as a result of a marketing strategy which has promoted it as a "must-have" item, or as a result of stock shortages.

hotlist *noun*
1. a list of objects/people currently in demand because they have been proclaimed **hot items** by the people who make/sell them/selves 2. A cynical way of creating/ maintaining high levels of inequality.

HR *noun*
1. Human Resources. 2. the human form of raw materials, minions who can be ordered around at will and reshaped to serve the purposes of the corporate beast (human resources can also be spent, thrown at problems and used up in the same way as other resources).

I

I hear what you say
1. I have *not* heard what you said. 2. I have no intention of listening to what you say, I merely pretended to listen to your nonsense. Now, keep quiet, and listen to mine.

immediate payoff *noun*
an immediate financial or other gain; a carrot to lure greedy investors, impatient for returns in the short term.

impactfulness *noun*
the quality of having an impact, e.g. instead of saying, much more cogently, that a particular presentation made an impression on an audience, one could say, "That excellent presentation had a high impactfulness."

implement *verb*
to execute, carry out, perform; put into effect; equip with tools. This is a word that is at the very heart of

businessspeak; successive new strategies are always **implemented**, for example, "The new **fast-track** strategy is to be **implemented** immediately company-wide."

implementation paradigms
ways of doing stuff.

improvement opportunities
1. problems; weaknesses. 2. ways, identified by management consultants, in which processes and performance can be improved. In pursuit of such improvements, individuals may be offered their own **improvement opportunities**, i.e. training courses. Those who fail to seize the opportunity presented to them to improve are likely to find themselves examining new employment opportunities.

incentivize *verb*
1. to offer an incentive, or incentives; to provide enticement or encouragement, e.g. "The sales force were **incentivized** by having the threat of the two weakest performers losing their jobs hanging over them," or, "The newly **incentivized** staff drove themselves on to break all existing production records." 2. to threaten, cajole, blackmail.

incremental *cf.* **excremental** *adjective*
1. of or pertaining to an increase or addition; of or pertaining to growth; of or pertaining to profit. 2. of a salary: a tiny, insignificant increase or addition, especially one of a series on a fixed scale; a regular increase in salary on such a scale.

increments *noun pl.*
1. small increases in profit, salary, etc. 2. addition; growth; gain. 3. tiny, seemingly insignificant changes that can gradually bring about a significant change.

incubate *verb*
1. to develop something (an egg/an infectious disease/an idea) slowly without outward or perceptible signs. 2. to sit on an idea, like a hen on an egg, until it's fully developed and can be **implemented**, e.g. "Having thoroughly **incubated** his idea, the boss unleashed his new strategy on the company." 3. to leave something to languish in the in-tray, quite possibly indefinitely.

incubation period *noun*
1. the time taken for an egg/infectious disease/idea to incubate. 2. time spent pondering an idea which will utterly transform the world, or your company, at the very least.

infomediaries *noun*
1. internet companies which gather and link information on particular subjects on behalf of commercial organizations and their potential **customers**. 2. informants, evil spies, and **phishers**; these are the reason why your inbox is full to overflowing each morning with offers to extend the length of your penis/provide you with a free laptop/or open up a Pandora's box of limitless, and unfathomable, porn.

infotainment *noun*
1. a form of entertainment combined with journalism developed to make broadcast material which is intended both to entertain and to inform, often used by 24-hour television news networks, designed to evoke sentimental emotional

responses from viewers in between actual news of national interest and importance. 2. the opposite of news.

initiative *noun*
1. the quality of being able to initiate, or begin, something; the power or opportunity to act before others do, e.g., "By **seizing the initiative** and getting out there a week ahead of his competitors the salesman/woman was able to capture the lion's share of the market." 2. a fresh strategy intended to resolve or improve something, usually **implemented** by power-hungry egomaniacs. 3. a new way in which to torment employees.

innovate *verb*
to make changes, bring in something new; change something established by introducing new methods, ideas, or **products**; often demanded by managers of their workers, that they should constantly innovate in order to improve the bottom line.

innovative *adjective*
1. mind-numbingly unoriginal, hackneyed, dully derivative. 2. *computer science* new features in a program which make it more irritating and less useful.

insourcing *verb*
the process of finding some sucker, or group of suckers, within the company, to tackle some task which the management can't find anyone foolish enough outside the company to take on; simply having to do yourself what you can't find adequately qualified people to do for a fee you can afford; doing something yourself, in-house, so that the costs don't show in the **budget**; the opposite of **outsourcing**.

integrate *verb*
1. to bring together into one office/company/computer system/etc. 2. to mix, merge, blend; join, unite; unite to form a whole; desegregate, bring together as equals regardless of race or religion (yeah, right!).

integration *noun*
the bringing together into one entity of various disparate parts, e.g., the merging of two companies, with workers coming together to share office space and resources (disintegration is the more normal result of such mergers).

intellectual capital *noun*
a term with various definitions according to different theories of economics; accordingly its only truly neutral definition is as a debate over the economic qualities of an individual or group of individuals, especially those organized in an official group (e.g., a sports team or office) which affect performance but are not readily observable. **Intellectual capital** is often cited as a reason for performance that is unexpectedly better, or worse, than expected.

interactive *adjective*
1. of two people or things influencing each other, the usual result being bad feeling. 2. of a computer or other electronic device responding to the user's input; workers shuffling round the internet when they are supposed to be working.

interdependently *adverb*
in a mutually dependent manner, somewhere between "independently" and "together" – nothing will happen unless everyone joins in. This works well when a group of

friends is splitting a bill in a restaurant, but less well when a group of people who hate each other are forced to collaborate on a large project.

interfaces *noun*
1. surfaces that form a common boundary between two bodies, equipment or programs which enable two different systems or programs to communicate, although if the constituent parts differ too widely, the end result can be catastrophic. 2. Commonly, the interface of each brain with the brains of everyone else when using the internet.

internal subjectivity *noun*
squabbles among work colleagues.

in the final analysis *cf*. **at the end of the day**
another meaningless tag, conveying nothing, e.g. "When all is said and done/**at the end of the day/in the final analsyis** our results this year have been good."

intransigent stance *noun*
an uncompromising position adopted by an unyielding person, the typical behaviour of a stubborn jerk.

introduction, who needs no
an expression used when introducing a complete nonentity in dire need of a compelling introduction, which is, in fact, about to be given, who has just used the above expression.

intuitive *adjective*
1. of using one's instincts rather than thinking something through; of intuiting a solution to a problem, rather than

analysing it and devising one. 2. of doing something inexplicably stupid.

intuitive technology *noun*
1. technology that is readily comprehensible simply by playing around with it to facilitate use of a technological device, software, website, cell phone, car stereo, paper shredder, etc. 2. technology that is almost entirely incomprehensible, even with reference to a manual.

issue *noun*
a critical word in the **businessspeak** lexicon since the end of the last century, as in, "This is not an **issue**," or, "This is a major **issue**." When an **issue** arises it needs to be considered, a decision must be made, and action must be taken. At that stage, the **issue** is regarded as having been addressed. **Issues** may also be **flagged** for future attention.

iterate *verb*
to say something, or to explain something for the first time, usually followed by reiteration: the same thing being repeated over and over again, ad nauseam.

I, there's no . . . in team
a cringeworthy depiction of the undesirability of individualism in teamwork. There is, however, an "i" in "initiative" – in fact, there are four of them, so chew on that, you dull little sheep.

J

job action *noun*
1. a temporary action, such as a slowdown or strike, by workers as a protest and means of forcing compliance with demands. 2. looking for another job.

job security *noun*
ho ho ho.

job surfer *noun*
an employee skilled at jumping ship and getting a better job elsewhere before his or her incompetence is exposed.

jumpative *adjective*
being in an excitable state of mind or being; eager to do something, typically descriptive of the behaviour of a new employee who has not yet succumbed to the cynicism of his or her co-workers.

jump on the devil *verb*
1. to escape from the police by pressing the accelerator to the floor; *office* to make a quick getaway from a vengeful boss. 2. to obey the devil on your one shoulder, rather than the angel on the other.

jump-start *verb*
to start or re-start vigorously, with the aid of an external power source, usually in a desperate attempt to rescue a failing project or company.

jump to it *verb*
hurry up and get on with it.

just add water *verb cf.* **oven-ready**
a favourite catchphrase of advertisers in the mid-twentieth century retreaded to suggest that a business scheme has been thoroughly developed and requires simply to be launched.

K

keeping your head down
1. taking care not to stand out from the crowd, either to avoid being chosen to perform a particular task, or as a way of hiding from someone, especially when you have done something wrong, in the hope that the storm will blow over. 2. an attempt, usually flawed, at temporary invisibility.

keep me posted *verb*
1. let me know how you're getting on. 2. get on with it, and don't bother me directly, just send me the odd bulletin. 3. go away, I've finished discussing this and would very much like to keep it at arm's length.

keep your nose to the grindstone
1. apply yourself conscientiously to your work. 2. you must continue working until someone allows you to stop.

key *adjective*
1. integral, extremely important, of that on which an entire enterprise hinges. 2. of a person or element of a project or process: eminently dispensable, often forgotten.

key success factors *noun pl.*
those factors that are a necessary condition for success in a given market; that is, a company which performs poorly with regard to even just one of the relevant **key success factors** is almost certain to fail.

kick off *verb*
in much the same way as meetings used to "begin," they now "**kick off**," making use of an expression borrowed from sport to convey dynamism and excitement, often sadly lacking in practice.

killer *adjective*
of an application/**product**/service which gives its software/company an overwhelming advantage in the marketplace, e.g. "The **killer** application incorporated in our software will deliver a knock-out blow to our competitors." The adjective is sometimes wishfully applied as **killer** applications, etc., can sometimes turn on themselves and commit *hara kiri*.

KISS
Keep It Simple, Stupid.

knock-on effect *noun*
a chain reaction, or series of reactions in which each is caused directly by the one before it; consequence, effect, outcome, result, event, **issue**, upshot. Never own up to having initiated a chain reaction; push that first domino and stand well clear.

knowledge architecture *noun*
infrastructure composed of people, content, and technology in an inseparable and interdependent matrix; a prerequisite for knowledge sharing. Hello? Okay, imagine one of those towers of people standing on each other's shoulders, like a house of cards, all thinking and talking to each other, or floors of office workers linked to each other by **e-mail** and telephones – that's the knowledge architecture of the company, like the building they're all in, but made up of the people inside. Just like bricks-and-mortar architecture, the **knowledge architecture** of a company can vary between a lowly hovel and a magnificent palace. Usually, the building it most closely represents is a clapboard bungalow.

knowledge base *noun*
1. a collection of facts and rules for solving problems. 2. a room full of people wondering what to do.

KPI *noun*
Key Performance Indicators: previously agreed, specific indicators as to whether an organization or an individual is doing well. The famous theatre KPI of "bums on seats," for example, is not concerned with whether those bums are still on the seats after the interval or even how much they paid to be there; as long as they're there, mission accomplished.

L

last, but not least
1. far and away the least significant aspect of a report/presentation/speech. 2. last, despite protestations to the contrary, because of least importance. 3. "Hang on! I nearly forgot this."

lateralled, to be *cf.* **career drift**
US to be moved sideways, without promotion, in a stagnating career; to be **flatlining**.

layoff *noun*
1. the practice used by marginally profitable companies to compensate for ineffective management by releasing people from their employment, as in, "Even after the **layoff**, the company could still not get into the black." 2. firing people.

leading edge *cf.* **state of the art**, **bleeding edge** *noun*
while more up-to-the-minute than the slightly tired **state of the art**, **leading edge** should be used with caution as some analysts regard it as being synonymous with **bleeding edge**, i.e., expensive to develop and prone to failure.

leading-edge *adjective*
1. of something which, it is claimed, has not existed previously. 2. marketing weasel-speak for something which is nominally innovative.

lessons learnt
1. the aftermath of a cock-up. 2. part of a technique to force workers to become reflective, and to "learn" from their achievements and mistakes, and those of others; reflection on events in a structured way in order to learn from what has happened (or what didn't happen). The **lessons are learnt** by writing things down and "reflecting" on them after work. While making stupid mistakes sometimes teaches one not to make those specific mistakes again, it unfortunately rarely teaches one not to be stupid.

leverage *noun*
1. a favourite of those in management, and those who aspire to be managers, **leverage** originally described the advantage gained by using a lever as a tool. It later came to be used to describe corporate debt, for example, a "leveraged buy-out" is one in which the buyer has to borrow money in order to purchase the target company. After much subsequent misuse, the word leverage no longer describes much at all and has little meaning to anyone who has ever worked in an office. 2. in **hedge funds**, leverage is a hallowed term, as, if you borrow a

large amount of money and make a small profit on it, you nevertheless make a great deal of money. Most **hedge fund** managers choose not to think about what happens when one borrows a large amount of money and makes a loss on it, which is why so many **hedge funds** are "here today and gone tomorrow."

logistics *noun*
1. the management of supply chains to control the flow of goods, energy, information, etc., from the source of production to the marketplace; this could be an enormous, critical function of a multinational corporation, or a man with a van, who describes what he does as **logistics**. 2. an excuse for failing to deliver on a promise.

Long Tail, The
describes a business model in which a company with an effective distribution network is able to sell a greater volume of otherwise hard-to-find items in small volumes, than popular items in large volumes. Books with a **long tail**, i.e. those which keep on selling in reasonable volumes if not spectacularly, are very useful to publishing companies in keeping their businesses afloat, as they throw money at their front lists.

long-term forecast *noun*
how much profit the directors will still be making long after you've been made redundant and had your pension fund liquidated by incompetent investors.

low-hanging fruit *noun*
1. easy pickings. 2. those performance/**sales targets** you can achieve without breaking a sweat.

More Bullshit Job Titles

Generate your own bullshit job title, or help someone else with theirs. Simply combine one word, chosen randomly, from each column to generate a new title.

Central	Response	Administrator
Global	Paradigm	Architect
Customer	Tactics	Analyst
Investor	Identity	Designer
Dynamic	Markets	Planner
International	Group	Orchestrator
Legacy	Division	Technician
Forward	Applications	Developer
Internal	Optimization	Producer
Human	Operations	Consultant

M

magnetic *adjective*
1. attractive, compelling, e.g., "This new ad campaign is so **magnetic** that consumers are falling over themselves to buy our **product**." 2. term used to describe an item of no obvious use.

management consultants *noun*
young upstarts who march into a company they've never worked for in an industry they don't understand, do a quick head count, then fire randomly in an ill-thought-out cost-cutting exercise – a bit like an aggrieved ex-colleague returning with a gun and going "loco," or "postal."

margin *noun*
1. fancy terminology for profit. 2. the pittance left over after the costs, which were underestimated, have been subtracted from the sales, which were overestimated.

marketing department *noun*
1. a gaggle of sycophants and networkers. 2. frustrated creative wannabes.

market penetration *noun*
macho terminology for the extent to which your company's "**product**" is out there; you may not have the market *share* yet, but at least you're making inroads if you've successfully penetrated that market – forcefully, ideally.

mass market *noun*
1. the market for goods that are produced in large quantities and the justification for the campaign of fear waged by the media, the oil barons, and the government intended to keep us enslaved by our possessions. 2. the market for cheapened and debased versions of a company's **products**; supermarkets and other outlets which refuse to pay a normal market price.

matrix management *noun*
1. conventional organizations are run from the top down with a clear hierarchy of command and control, while **matrix** organizations assemble "functional" teams which draw some members from line management, who contribute while continuing to perform their line functions. 2. one of the more recent bandwagons of management theory to have trundled past attracting the **fad surfers**.

maximize *verb*
1. to make as large or great as possible. 2. to make the best possible use of something which is possibly deficient, or defective, e.g., "In order to **maximize** his potential, Ray attended numerous part-time courses after work."

mentee *noun*

a person who is advised, trained, bullied, abused, and then counselled by a **mentor**.

mesh *noun*

the result of putting together a lot of disparate persons/**products** and trying to make them fit together.

mesh *verb*

to entangle or entwine, or to become entangled or entwined with; either way, the end result can be violence.

methodology *noun*

a system of methods used in a particular field; a way of getting things done, or not.

metrics *noun*

1. a means of measuring something, usually performance in the workplace. 2. Are you doing your job? Properly?

metrosexual *noun*

1. a straight, but trendy, city guy, who, on clothes and grooming alone, could be mistaken for a gay guy. 2. a still closeted gay guy. 3. an unfortunate target for various **products** ranging from terrible magazines to terrible clothes.

micromanagement *noun*

a management strategy that entails interference in every single aspect of employees' lives. A **micromanager** may go as far as to ask employees to keep detailed journals of every action each one of them undertakes. The best way for employees to fight back is to keep a journal in which each ten-minute block contains the entry, "Filled in my

journal reporting on the previous ten minutes of work."
This will either result in them leaving you alone, or in
your being fired, which, in the face of **micromanagement**, would be a positive relief.

milestone *noun*
1. a significant stage or event in the development of
something en route to a target, often attained with a sense of
relief in the workplace, though usually it marks only a small
plateau before the climb begins again. 2. an unreasonable
half-way or other goal set by management.

mind-map *noun*
1. a diagram representing ideas, tasks, etc., arranged on
spokes around a central key idea used to help solve
problems and make decisions. 2. a spidery scrawl
contributing to fuzzy thinking.

mindset *noun*
a person's mental disposition which determines, to a large
extent, his or her responses to situations. Management
prides itself on understanding **mindsets**, knowing how
particular people will behave in any given situation. Thus
equipped, bosses are able to exert thought control on the
"defective" **mindsets** of their employees; this supposed
understanding of thought processes rarely extends to their
own.

mindshare *noun*
consumer awareness of a **product** or **brand**, as opposed
to market share (which is dependent on consumers
actually buying a **product**, rather than simply having
heard of it), and nothing to do with two or more people
sharing a single mind (in the same kind of way as jobshare

denotes two or more people sharing a single job).

mission-critical *adjective*
a gift to businessspeak from NASA's space program; to be used when the success or failure of an entire enterprise rests on certain **mission-critical** tasks – to fail in any one of these would be to condemn a mission to abject failure.

mission statement *noun*
1. intended to assist all employees in focusing on the key goals of the company, usually prominently displayed around them. 2. a statement of intent. 3. a ludicrous farrago of bland pronouncements suitable only to be jeered at by employees during bitch-and-moan sessions.

modular organization *noun*
an organization in which different functional components are separated from one another, usually by Chinese, i.e. non-existent walls, so, for example, those doing the investing still know what those doing the advising are telling their clients, despite whatever management might claim to the contrary.

moment *noun*
1. an indefinitely short period of time; an instant. 2. a delaying tactic, as in, "I'll be with you in a **moment**." 3. Now, as in, **at this moment in time**.

monetize *verb*
1. to devise some way to make money from what your company does, so, rather than having no revenue at all, some money begins to trickle in. 2. to become cripplingly indebted by borrowing against your company's real assets

in pursuit of imaginary growth. 3. to **monetize the clicks** is a quixotic attempt to make money from a website, especially relevant for a company which doesn't actually have anything to sell online but somehow imagined that a web presence would be profitable.

morph *verb*
1. to transform smoothly from one thing into another, e.g., "I've had a varied career and **morph** easily into something new every couple of years." 2. shorthand for the drug morphine, as in, "The CEO wants to re-organize all the departments at the same time. It may be time for some **morph**."

movers and shakers *noun*
the most significant people in a team, company, or marketplace – they move and shake while others duck and dive. Also: **key players**.

moving the goalposts *verb*
to unfairly alter the conditions or rules of a procedure during its course, used by pernickety bosses who keep changing their mind about what they have told you to do.

multitask *verb*
1. the execution of more than one program or task simul-taneously by sharing resources. 2. something which women have been doing successfully for millennia, but which men seem ill-equipped to master.

N

net present value *noun*
1. a standard method for the financial evaluation of long-term projects, **net present value** is future cashflows in today's value set against a discount factor minus the initial investment. If the **net present value** of cumulative cashflows is positive, then the project should be accepted, unless a more profitable investment is also available.
2. Should we do it, or not?

network *verb/noun*
updated version of the "Old Boys' Club" in which being old and male are not prerequisites; the primary purpose of a **network** is to place acquaintances and social skills before merit, education, skills, and knowledge in career advancement.

new economy *noun*
1. the evolution of developed countries from industrial/manufacture-based, wealth-producing economies into

service sector, wealth-consuming, asset-based economies, with fewer job opportunities for the middle class, arising partly from the overvaluation of technology stocks and partly from **globalization** and currency manipulation by governments and their central banks. However, as we all know, this all went horribly wrong when the **dot-com** bubble burst. 2. an economy which differs from whatever was in place before.

next-generation *adjective*
1. the next best thing. 2. the same as the old generation, though with a handful of additional, irritating features.

next level *noun*
1. better than what went before; an improvement on existing technology/processes/companies/etc., e.g., "By implementing our new "Go Faster" strategy we will take the services offered by our delivery company to the **next level**." A borrowing from the world of computer games involving a progression from one level to the next. 2. one step closer to unimpeachable excellence.

niche *noun*
1. an area of the market that specializes in one type of **product** or service, usually something wacky, new age or luxury that not many people want, or can afford. 2. **niche** *adjective* of a position or activity that especially suits a particular individual's talents and personality, or which an individual can make his or her own; of a bona fide weirdo.

NIH
Not Invented Here; any **product** or procedure brought into a company from outside or **implemented** from the top down with little or no consultation; an explanation for

limited enthusiasm on the part of employees for adopting such a **product** or procedure.

no-blame culture *noun*
these days, when something goes wrong, instead of looking for a scapegoat to blame, an executive will say something like, "I just want to understand how we can avoid this scenario in future." Once he or she understands, and the scapegoat has been flushed out, he or she is fired.

no-brainer *cf.* **rocket science** *noun*
1. readily understandable, even by dolts, the complete opposite of **rocket science**. 2. a course of action so clear that no further time should be wasted thinking about it.

nominal growth *cf.* **real growth** *noun*
growth defined only in terms of a depreciating currency; **nominal growth** often goes hand in hand with losses which are all too real.

non-delegated *adjective*
of a task which has not been assigned to anyone, because no one suitable could be found, or because the delegator has not yet got around to it; it implies forethought, as if the task has been left deliberately unassigned. "This is a non-delegated task." ("You're on your own with this one.")

no one rings a bell at the top
no one tells you when stocks have peaked; if you wait for an announcement of some kind instructing you to sell, you'll have missed the boat – a good line to use, smugly, in passing, to someone who has missed his or her opportunity to sell for the highest possible price.

not a problem
1. easy; unproblematic. 2. "I haven't heard a word you've just said, I'm thinking of something else and I'm coming up with some meaningless stock phrase in an attempt to reassure you that your very real problem is no big deal and will somehow be sorted." 3. a problem.

not-trivial *adjective*
difficult, but sounds more "in control" than saying, "This is impossible," or "This is frying my mind."

off balance sheet
1. of an asset or debt which is not on the company's balance sheet, which should show all assets and liabilities; these could be leases, subsidiary companies, letters of credit, loan commitments, etc. 2. a dubious accounting practice, whereby various loopholes are used to prevent expenses from showing up on the company balance sheet.

off-line *adjective*
1. disconnected from the internet. 2. outside this meeting. 3. of a confidential bit of gossip, e.g., "This is **off-line**, of course, you can't tell anyone." 4. asleep at one's desk.

off-site meeting *noun*
1. a form of meeting designed to "shake things up" by getting employees away from their desks; a team-bonding adventure day/weekend. 2. an employee bitchfest in a restaurant, café, bar, etc. – these work best when either the company credit card is being used, or the money can be claimed back as a work-related expense.

one-minute manager *noun*
1. a manager who subscribes to the **one-minute management** theory and will refuse to listen to any degree of detail or explanation, simply making an arbitrary decision within a maximum of 60 seconds. 2. a bored, or lazy, manager, one who can't be bothered.

one-off *adjective*
1. of something which will take place just once, as in, "This is a **one-off** opportunity; I won't be able to offer you the same price again!" 2. same old, same old.

one-off *noun*
something that is unique, one of a kind; there's nothing out there quite like it.

on the runway
1. ready to go, like an aeroplane revving its engines before take-off. 2. the high point of any project, the moment when all the work has been done, but potential flaws are yet to be exposed.

on the same page *cf.* **get on the same page**
1. on the same piece of paper. 2. of two colleagues, that they are are moving in roughly the same direction as each other, in pursuit of broadly the same goal (in fact, the chances that they are even "in the same library" are usually fairly remote).

open question *noun*
1. an **open question** requires a descriptive answer, e.g., the question, "Do you prepare purchase orders?" could be answered with a simple yes or no, whereas, "How do you prepare purchase orders?" requires more information. An

open question can present a minefield for the unwary, exposing those with a careless tongue to harsh judgment. 2. the answer is not known, as in, "That's an **open question**." ("We haven't a clue.")

operationalize *verb*
to put into practice, to make something happen; to put into operation. Another bastardized form of a word filched from a military context, e.g. Operation Desert Storm, it aims to give the impression of something overpowering and brutally effective, qualities conveyed by the ugliness of the word itself.

opportunity *noun*
1. a problem (it would be too weak-kneed to acknowledge an obstacle or a setback; these are merely **opportunities for improvement**, or learning **opportunities**). 2. something to be seized with both hands, e.g., "When **opportunity** knocks, you need to throw open the door and embrace it, so that, together, you can set off down the sunny side of the street."

opportunity for improvement
1. a terrible situation, a calamity; a time for self-criticism. When a boss describes something as an **opportunity for improvement**, you have clearly screwed up, big time, and the inference is that it is time to shape up, or ship out. 2. your job is on the line.

optimize *verb*
to make something as good as it can be; to modify a system to make some aspect of it work more efficiently, supposedly, or use fewer resources (ironically, **optimization** usually results in job cuts or increased misery in one form or another during the working day).

opt-in *adjective*
1. **opt-in e-mail** is mail which one has opted somehow to receive, by joining a mailing list, subscribing to a newsletter, or agreeing to receive advertising. If the sender has not obtained permission, such mailings are known as "unsolicited bulk **e-mail**," or, more commonly, spam. 2. of spam, received as a result of inadvertently providing some organization with your details, or missing some well camouflaged tick-box, often already ticked and needing unticking.

opt-out *adjective*
of several methods by which individuals can avoid receiving unsolicited **e-mails**, or spam. Be warned, though, that an **opt-out** with one marketer seems to be an automatic **opt-in** with another. There is no escape.

orchestrate *verb*
to play the composer, bending many diverse talents to your will; to be the master of all, overseeing everyone playing in harmony, performing your bidding, e.g., "Through a clever campaign of media manipulation, posturing, and bullying, the chief trade negotiator succeeded in **orchestrating** a beneficial trade agreement."

out-of-the-box *adjective*
of non-conformist, creative thinking, supposedly derived from a famous puzzle created by twentieth-century British mathematician Henry Dudeney, which requires nine dots in a three-by-three grid to be connected by using four straight lines, drawn without the pencil leaving the paper. For this to be done successfully, the person solving the puzzle has to realize that the boundaries of the square formed by the dot matrix must be broken; he or she needs

to employ **out-of-the-box** thinking. A likely tale which is probably more creative than most of what passes for **out-of-the-box** thinking in large corporations.

out of the loop
1. uninvolved. 2. shut out. 3. excluded. 4. shunned. 5. unloved.

outsource *verb*
1. to purchase goods or subcontract services from an outside supplier or source. 2. to have **products** made in far-off sweatshops by young children working twelve-hour days, seven days a week, in unsanitary conditions. 3. to fire people.

oven-ready *adjective cf.* **just add water**
a contractor or consultant is said to be **oven-ready** when he or she is ready to go with no training and minimum briefing, as in, "We have an army of **oven-ready** consultants ready to unleash on your company; we can **operationalize** them in an instant."

overview *noun cf.* **big picture**
the god-like perspective of one who is master of all he or she surveys; the eagle's-eye view of prey scurrying pathetically and hopelessly in the exposed grassland of the marketplace; the opposite of a nuts-and-bolts grasp of the nitty-gritty.

P

paper fortune *noun*
vast wealth created by accounting sleight of hand, easily dissipated by accurate auditing.

paradigm *noun*
a thought pattern; a way of doing things.

paradigm blindness *noun*
1. "We're doing it this way because it's the way we've always done it." 2. stubbornness, pigheadedness.

paradigm shift *noun*
taking thinking to the **next level**.

partner *noun*
1. a person who shares or is associated with another in some action or endeavour; sharer; associate. 2. one of the lucky few who work about an hour a week, yet have

bigger houses, better cars, and longer, more exotic holidays than most of us could ever aspire to.

partnership *noun*
1. the state or condition of being a partner; participation; association; joint interest. 2. a pack of **partners**, all of them enjoying bigger houses, better cars, etc.

passion *noun*
1. any powerful or compelling emotion or feeling, such as love or hate. 2. what corporations promise with regard to their **product** (from information technology to pork scratchings), and demand of their employees, no matter how mundane their job, as in, "Applicants should have a **passion** for photocopying. No chancers."

path to profitability, **P2P** *noun*
1. a business plan designed to take an enterprise from being a start-up to turning a profit. 2. a good nugget of jargon to trot out when presenting your business plan to your bank manager, as in, "With our rock solid **P2P** we see ourselves being in the black before the year is out."

payroll adjustment *noun*
1. the process of adjusting someone's pay, usually downwards, sometimes retroactively. **Payroll adjustments** are very, very rarely in an upward direction. 2. adjusting the payroll by removing people from it; firing people.

peeling the onion *verb*
1. getting to the bottom of something, or to the heart of the matter; usually some kernel of fault will be exposed and

blame can then be apportioned. 2. A laborious process which usually ends in tears.

peer group *noun*
1. a group of people sharing roughly the same age, social status, and interests. 2. a support system for professionals, helping them to better understand themselves so that they can better serve their patients/clients. 3. a group of meddling busybodies getting in the way and getting on your nerves with their "no fixing, no advising, no setting each other straight" rubric. Go it alone!

peer-to-peer, **P2P** *adjective*
1. of computer networks in which each computer is connected to each other computer, rather than to a central server or servers, useful for sharing files, particularly those containing audio or video data. 2. a rat run in cyber-space enabling copyright material to be shunted round, relatively free of scrutiny, and virtually immune from policing.

performance-related pay, **PRP** *noun*
1. financial reward commensurate with inexperience and/or incompetence. 2. subsistence-level basic pay to be "topped up" according to a complex formula, or not, depending on how well you do.

phisher *noun*
someone who attempts, criminally and fraudulently, to acquire sensitive information, such as usernames, passwords, and credit card details, by masquerading as a trustworthy entity in an electronic communication. This is usually done by sending crudely designed and badly spelled **e-mails** demanding bank account numbers,

passwords, usernames, addresses, dates of birth and mothers' maiden names because your bank is updating its system. Only a real phish would respond.

photoblog *noun*
a constantly updated website jam-packed with sickly, sentimental, or self-consciously "wacky" images.

pinch point *noun*
1. the point in a piece of machinery where there is risk of getting a body part caught and crushed. 2. a position in a business transaction, or within a corporation, where you may find yourself caught, trapped, and crushed.

pipeline *noun*
the place where things which are about to happen, but not happening yet, exist, believed by some to be a mythical place, as in, "Where is that report I asked you to compile last month?" "It's in the **pipeline**" ("I haven't started it yet").

place a premium on *verb*
to put an unusually high value on something in order to get people to pay more or work harder, as in, "This company **places a premium on** loyalty (but will lay you off as soon as look at you)."

plate, a lot on my
1. busy. 2. swamped. 3. had enough. 4. heading for a nervous breakdown.

platform *noun*
1. a surface which supports objects, gives them stability, or increased visibility. 2. the basic technology of a computer system's hardware and software which defines

how a computer is operated and determines what other kinds of software can be used; often inherently unstable; also used by large software manufacturers to exclude the **products** of smaller companies by ensuring that they are not compatible with their platforms.

plug-and-play *adjective*
1. of a device such as a scanner or printer that can, in theory, be linked to a computer without having to recon-figure the hard drive or manually instal device drivers; more normally **plug-fiddle about endlessly-replug-and-play**. 2. of temporary staff: their ability to adapt seamlessly to an existing work environment, or not.

plutoed, to be
to be summarily demoted in the same way that Pluto recently lost its status as a planet of our solar system, e.g., "Following his disappointing appraisal, no one was surprised when Ray was **plutoed**."

podcast *noun*
a terrible piece of internet journalism made by amateur presenters about completely inconsequential issues.

podcast *verb*
to pretend to be telling the public about something inter-esting and important when, in reality, you simply like the sound of your own voice.

podcatcher *adjective*
1. software in a computer which downloads and organizes podcasts for transfer to a digital music player. 2. a filter feeder in cyberspace seeking the world's foolery and funneling it towards you.

portal *noun*
1. a "supersite" on the Web that provides a variety of services such as a search function, news, free **e-mail**, discussion groups, shopping, and links to other sites. 2. a magical entrance to another world filled with wonder (*archaic*).

positioning *noun*
where a **brand** or **product** is placed in the marketplace; how potential buyers see the **product**; a desperate attempt to enhance the desirability of a **brand** or **product** by implying that it is in some way a quality or luxury item.

power-shifting
1. changing gear without taking your foot off the accelerator. 2. making the transition to a more powerful computer system with no down-time. 3. moving from one task to another with no let-up in speed or efficiency, the preferred transition mode of the Masters of the Corporate World.

primary takeaway *noun*
the main point to be taken from a particular meeting or conference; usually a feeling of emptiness, a void.

principle-centred *adjective*
of actions, leadership, policies, etc., which remain true to a set of principles, for example, one version of **principle-centred** leadership might attempt to place environmental concerns at the heart of a company's practices; an alternative to, for example, rapaciously profit-centred actions/ leadership/policies, etc.

prior to
before, but sounds better, more formal, doesn't it?

proactive *adjective*
of empowered, self-reliant actions, individuals, etc.; an antonym of **reactive**, merely reacting to events as they unfold, rather than shaping events autonomously. Businesses like proactive individuals, people who take initiative, seize the day, rather than mere fire-fighters, pathetically attempting to douse flames lit by others.

process-flow *noun*
1. the **key** chain of events in getting from A to B. 2. the flow of photocopied documents, memos, and **e-mails** from one person to another, initiated in the vague hope that something might occur as a result of them.

product *noun*
1. object that is manufactured in factories (*archaic*). 2. object that is imported from factories thousands of miles away. 3. anything, manufactured or otherwise, that can be flogged for money.

productful *adjective*
Anything wrong with the existing word "productive"? Anyone? Anyone?

productionized *adjective*
of something which has advanced from undergoing tests to actually being produced; of something which has "gone live." Another jewel of **corporatese**, a word to curl the tongue around.

productivity *noun*

the value of goods or services produced over a period of time divided by the hours of labour used to produce them. It is a good idea to maintain a delicate balance with regard to one's personal **productivity**; being over-zealous simply increases the demands made by management.

productize *verb*

to turn something into a **product** in order to be able to sell it, for example, a large soft-drink manufacturer filling bottles with tap water, giving it a name, and attempting to sell it. Although that particular effort was not a success, similar things go on almost daily all around the world.

product life cycle *noun*

the succession of stages which a **product** goes through in the course of its lifetime, from its introduction, to growth in demand for the product, the maturity, or peak, of that demand, decline in demand, and withdrawal of the product from the market place. In some cases, this takes place over years or decades; in others, a new product can blaze through the marketplace and out the other end in the twinkling of an eye.

product manager *noun*

has full responsibility for, but little authority over, a particular product line.

projection *noun*

1. a dreamworld. 2. a wishful assessment of sales figures, profit, market share, etc., over a particular length of time; almost inevitably wrong, and often wilfully distorted.

pushback *noun*
a euphemism for a retreat, for example, when a **product** is withdrawn from the marketplace due to consumer resistance, as in, "Downward pressure has been exerted on our sales due to **pushback** in the marketplace."

putting out fires *verb*
instead of being **proactive** and **seizing** the initiative, scurrying around dealing with one minor calamity after another, as in, "I haven't had a moment to strategize, all I've been doing is running around **putting out fires**."

put to bed *verb*
to complete a task, as in, "Come on, let's **put this baby to bed** so we can go out and get wasted."

Q

quality control *noun*
the process of ensuring that all **products** are manufactured to an acceptable standard; the process of filtering out
obvious errors of judgment (rarely succesful).

quality-driven *adjective*
quality is in the driving seat, yes sir, profit is merely a
passenger; of **products**, processes, etc., where quality is
the *sine qua non*.

quick fix
1. a half-assed attempt at fixing a problem which usually
results in a bigger problem that could have been avoided
by doing the job properly first time around. 2. no fix at all.

quick status *noun*
at-a-glance information regarding who is online, what
they are doing and so on, sometimes provided by means
of a pop-up box activated by a mouse rolling over an item

on screen. No doubt shortly to **morph** into wikistatus or something similar, as part of being **productized** and sold.

quick win *noun*

an early positive result for an initiative or project; in the context of first aid, for example, "If we go for the **quick win** of lifting the breeze block off his chest, he'll be able to breathe again; then we can splint his broken leg," or, with regard to public transport, "If we aim for the **quick win** of getting the trains running again, we can fine-tune the time-table in due course."

Yet More Bullshit Job Titles

Generate your own bullshit job title, or help someone else with theirs. Simply combine one word, chosen randomly, from each column to generate a new title.

Chief	Infrastructure	Assistant
Principle	Intranet	Facilitator
Lead	Communications	Agent
Senior	Web	Representative
Direct	Branding	Strategist
Corporate	Quality	Supervisor
Central	Assurance	Associate
Global	Mobility	Executive
Customer	Accounts	Liaison
Investor	Data	Co-ordinator

R

rainmaker *noun*
1. someone who brings new business to a team, or company, and shares a similar status to a shaman who brings rain to a community dependent on rainfall for their crops.
2. someone who is on friendly terms with a lot of people in his or her industry, often through family connections.

raising the bar
demanding higher levels of performance. Just as a high jumper has to keep clearing the bar at ever-increasing heights to stay in the competition, businesses and individuals need to keep redoubling their efforts to clear the bar which has been raised either by management or competitors. Usually, just as one has finally managed to clear the bar, it is raised, resulting in failure all over again.

ramp up *verb*
increase. Why use one word when you can use two?

random sampling *noun*
a pick-and-mix approach to **quality control**.

reactive *adjective*
1. of someone who is constantly **putting out fires**, merely reacting to events and crises, rather than intitiating things.
2. of someone who sits and does nothing until told to do something; opposite of **proactive**.

real growth *cf.* **nominal growth** *noun*
growth of the kind constantly demanded by stock-holders, far in excess of other companies, of the sort that if every company in the world experienced **real growth** for a few decades, every possible resource in the world would be vacuumed up and destroyed in the name of perpetual growth.

real-time *adjective*
of telephone conversations between people in different time zones, as opposed to voicemail and **e-mail** messages, as in, "We need to arrange to have a **real-time** conversation about this."

recontextualize *verb*
1. to frame a problem differently to give it the appearance of being more manageable. 2. to view a problem in the light of a **paradigm shift**. 3. to rephrase something, as in, "Let me **recontextualize** that for you. When I said that we would be **right-sizing** the team, what I meant was that you are fired."

redefine *verb*
1. to give an old dog a new name. 2. to attempt to improve dramatically something which you know to be rubbish.

redeployed people *noun pl.*
an aimless, shuffling mass of people being shunted from pillar to post, removed from their usual posts and placed in other, often temporary, and as often inferior posts, such as making tea/coffee, shredding documents, and buying lunch for the directors.

reintermediate *verb*
1. to remove intermediaries from a **supply chain**; to cut out the middleman. 2. to set up a direct marketing company on the internet, for example, with minimal staff and limited floor-space requirements. 3. to lust after more money.

reinvent the wheel *verb*
to ignore existing, cost-effective technological solutions to a problem you may be confronting in favour of doing all the work of devising something yourself; more broadly, to ignore affordable, existing processes, techniques, components, etc., in favour of doing everything your own way, even if you have to invest a huge amount of effort in producing something which already exists and is available to you. There is an infinitely better way, as in, "Let's not **reinvent the wheel**; lets go out and steal somebody else's wheels."

reorient *verb*
to brainwash.

reorienting *noun*
the process of twisting the mind of someone who is opposed to your ideas or actions; getting their **ducks in a row**, as it were.

reposition *verb*
in desperation, to shift the position of a **brand** or **product**
in the marketplace in the hope of convincing a different
group of suckers to buy it; products may be shifted
upmarket or downmarket, in whichever direction
consumers look more likely to bite. For example,
Marlborough cigarettes were initially pitched at female
consumers, before being **repositioned** to appeal to macho
men.

repurpose *verb*
another attractive, **corporatese** invention, meaning to
give something a new purpose or to use something in a
different manner, as in, "We feel that your talents are
wasted sitting in front of a computer; we are going to
repurpose you as a security guard."

research *verb*
1. to steal ideas from competitors. 2. to cut and paste.

resource levelling *noun*
1. a process which assesses whether a project is using
resources (usually people) in an unbalanced way over
time and which resolves over-allocations or other
conflicts; checking that resources are not being squan-
dered in order to boost profits. 2. as a boss, if you become
aware of too many staff standing around gossiping, fire
some of them.

response time *noun*
a macho measure of the time taken to complete a task, or
respond to an instruction or request, intended to conjure
up images of firemen sliding down poles and police cars
racing through city streets with their sirens on.

restructure *verb*
1. to change or reorganize a corporation in a way which allows employees to be fired at will while simultaneously stripping them of their right to sue for unlawful termination. 2. to fire or to make redundant.

restructuring *noun*
1. a euphemistic description of a process whereby workers can be fired, their pay lowered, and their conditions of employment altered for the worse. 2. changing the corporate structure of a company, particularly slimming it down if it has become, in the view of the bosses, a little "bottom-heavy."

result-driven *adjective*
of pay, an individual, a company, etc., when results are in the driving seat, as in, "We operate a **result-driven** pay structure here; if you perform well, you will be well rewarded."

retrosexual *noun*
a man's man, decidedly not a **metrosexual**: hairy, sweary, a hard drinker, into sports, that sort of thing; basically a man of retro habits.

reverse engineer *verb*
to steal someone else's idea by taking apart a **product** to understand how it works and how it was made, and copying it.

revisit *verb*
to visit again; to return to, as in, "Let's **revisit** that decision to **outsource** delivery because it seems to have sent our sales into freefall." Many bosses, for example,

will repeatedly **revisit** their pet ideas, despite their having failed persistently in the past due to their idiocy and unfeasibility.

revolutionize *verb*
1. to bring about immediate, drastic change, often with the use of violence, for example, "Management has **revolutonized** working conditions; from today employees will be paid substantially less for working much longer hours." 2. *advertising* used to make spurious, hubristic claims about the supposedly transformative nature of new **products**, e.g., "CheesyStix have **revolutionized** lunchtime for schoolchildren!"

right-sizing *noun*
1. trimming an organization down to its optimal fighting weight – the "right" size in question is seldom any bigger than the current size. 2. firing people.

risk management *noun*
1. the technique or profession of assessing, minimizing, and preventing accidental loss to a business, as through the use of insurance, safety measures, etc. 2. taking care to cover one's tracks to avoid being blamed for anything, ever.

robust *noun*
1. able to withstand stresses, pressures, or changes in procedure or circumstance. A system, organism, or design may be said to be **robust** if it is capable of coping well with variations (sometimes unpredictable variations) in its operating environment with minimal damage, alteration, or loss of functionality. 2. a doormat, which holds up well to being stood on, repeatedly, by many different people.

robust *adjective*
1. forceful, resilient, as in, "He mounted a **robust** defence of his deplorable track record, but to no avail. He was still fired." 2. of people who cannot control their weight; a euphemism for chubby, portly, fat. 3. of someone who is "up front and personal," both physically and vocally, in every conversation, especially when alcohol is involved. 4. downright rude and aggressive.

rocket science *cf.* **no-brainer** *noun*
a term of approbation for anything considered overly complex by the average Luddite or **technopeasant**; a task requiring above-average intelligence and technical ability, often used in the negative as a condescending put-down, as in, "It's not **rocket science**! Even a child could understand!"

runaround *noun*
see **wild goose chase**.

run the numbers (on) *verb*
to do some calculations in the hope that what is otherwise readily apparent will resolve itself into an altogether happier scenario, as in, "Let me **run the numbers on** that feeble offer in the forlorn hope that it might suddenly appear to be a good thing."

S

sacred cow *noun*
something which may not be questioned or challenged, usually something like a pet project of the boss, which should be regarded as sacrosanct, no matter how costly or foolish it might be.

sales force *noun*
a loosely aligned group of men and women responsible for flogging a company's **products**; the term "force" is used in the hope of mimicking qualities of tight-knit and highly effective organizations such as the Special Air Service, or the Navy SEALs.

salesperson *noun*
a member of the **sales force**; a free-ranging desperado of the commercial world, struggling always to meet his or her **sales target**.

sales report *noun*
1. report on sales made and projected. 2. a fictional account of sales made, and hopelessly optimistic projection of future sales.

sales target *noun*
1. the quantity of a particular **product** that a company expects to sell in the course of a year, or some other period. 2. a wildly optimistic estimate of revenue based on the projections of fantasists in the **sales force**.

scalable *adjective*
of something easily altered in size, as in, "The beauty of this project is that it is more or less infinitely **scalable**; we can allow it to balloon to the point where it begins to eat up all our resources, or we can trim it down to next to nothing," or, "Bear in mind that your work load is **scalable**; I can increase it at will."

scale *noun*
a device, designed to be stood on, commonly stored in the bathroom, which many people fear to step on.

scale *verb*
to make bigger, or smaller, as in "**scale** up" and "**scale** down."

scenario *noun*
1. a situation; the chain of events giving rise to a situation. 2. an imaginary situation, devised for the purposes of planning.

schema *noun*
a specific, well-documented, and consistent plan, as

opposed to a scheme, which is merely the outline of a plan; a model, a diagram. Be wary when the bosses begin to use the word **schema**; a scheme or idea has come to fruition, and is shortly to be **implemented**.

scope *noun*
the extent or range of something, as in, "What is the scope of this investigation into our books?" or, "This project is so wide-ranging in **scope** that you will be hard at it for months to come; say goodbye to your families now."

seize *verb*
1. to take quick and forcible possession of something, often used in conjunction with **opportunity**. 2. to grasp, or confiscate, something which belongs to someone else.

self-motivated *adjective*
driven, focused; of someone who bangs his head against changing-room lockers to psyche himself up before a sales drive or a **mission-critical** meeting; someone who is both coach and star player in his own little team.

self-starter *noun*
someone with get-up-and-go, who needs no further motivation to "pick up the ball and run with it"; a favourite in employment ads, as in, "**Dynamic self-starter** required for busy office. Earning potential limit-less." ("You're on your own here, so you'll need lots of energy. You will not be paid a basic salary, so it is possible that you may earn nothing in a given month.")

service-oriented *adjective*
pointed in the general direction of service – not actually providing it, mind, but "oriented" in that general direction.

sexy *adjective*
sexually attractive or alluring; of something that corporate suits see as attractive, appealing, or interesting, as in, "Emerging market stocks are very **sexy** at the moment," or, "Is there some way in which we could make this dossier more **sexy**?"

shoeshine-boy moment *noun*
the moment when one realizes that, since everybody thinks that stocks (or property or gold, or whichever asset is the subject of the latest bubble) can only ever go up, the crash will soon be upon us.

show-stopper *noun*
the absence of a **mission-critical** item, without which the show simply cannot go on.

silo *cf.* **flag** *verb*
1. to store something for future use or discussion; to store, like grain in a silo, as in, "Great idea! Why don't you **silo** that and we'll **revisit** it in the next meeting." 2. to put something where it will never be found again.

sing from the same hymn sheet
to work together, seamlessly, sharing the same objective and the same strategy, with everyone pulling together. With a suggestion of harmony. And joy.

skill-set *noun*
an individual's set of skills which are transferable from one role to another. An abundant **skill-set** is usually an asset to a company, seldom to an individual, as one individual can be required to do the work of two or more people.

slippery slope *noun*
a situation which degenerates rapidly and inexorably into a breakneck downhill run, from one disaster to another, as in, "If we're found to have simply bottled tap-water *and* it's contaminated, our sales will be on a **slippery slope**."

SME *noun*
1. Small or Medium Enterprise, a non-behemoth of the business world. 2. obscurantist jargon to keep outsiders and newcomers at bay, in the dark.

smell test *noun*, also **run it up the flagpole**
1. a way of assessing the potential for success of a particular **product**, as in, "I'm not convinced that that will work, but let's do a smell test, let's sniff it and see." 2. asking a few dozy people in the immediate vicinity what they think of your new idea.

smirt *verb*
to flirt while smoking outside an office building, restaurant, or bar.

smirt *noun*
someone who flirts while smoking outside an office building, restaurant, or bar, as in, "That man from the accountacy firm on the third floor is such a **smirt**, but he's getting nowhere with me. I've decided to give up smoking."

smirting *noun*
the act of attempting to flirt with people while smoking outside a building, probably huddled against pouring rain and icy cold with a bit of ash clinging to your cheek.

solution *noun cf.* **product** *archaic*
a **product** supplied by, or a service provided by a
company; the answer to your prayers, the way to solve
your problem. These days, nine out of ten companies,
instead of providing services or supplying **products**,
provide **solutions**. The following are examples of various
"**solution** providers," along with how we might once have
known them: Accomodation Solutions (flats/apartments);
Outsourced Vehicle Movement Solutions (car deliveries);
Envelope Solutions (envelopes); Integrated Vegetable
Supply Solutions (greengrocers); Post Office Mailing
Solutions (brown paper); Chilled Food Solutions (ready-
meals/convenience foods).

spearhead *verb*
to take the lead; to act as point man; to drive a project
forward, as in, "I admire your drive. I'd like you to **spearhead** the project to upgrade our logistics systems."

squaring the circle *verb*
doing something impossible – a problem posed by ancient
mathematicians relating to the areas of a square and a
circle was proved in the late nineteenth century to be
insoluble, hence the expression, as in, "It should be
possible to get out there and sell at least some of this fine
product! We're not **squaring the circle** here!"

staff reduction *noun*
mass firing.

state of the art *cf.* **leading edge**, **bleeding edge** *noun*
an expression used by lazy journalists for a technological
device which they do not fully understand, but believe to
be in the vanguard of development.

state-of-the-art *adjective*
of technology not fully understood but believed to be in the vanguard of development, as in, "The WonderGizmo Corporation recently unveiled a **state-of-the-art** digital reading tablet."

strategic *adjective*
1. to do with strategy; of something which does not seem to have a clear purpose, or seems unlikely to bring any short-term benefit, as in, "Investing in our internet presence at this stage is a purely **strategic** move; we do not expect to recoup much of our expenditure." 2. of something which has failed, attempting to provide some justification, as in, "Our move into real estate was purely **strategic**, intended only to give us a presence in the sector rather than any significant market share." ("Our move into real estate has been an abject failure.")

strategic initiative *noun*
a cunning, well-thought-out plan that has been **implemented**, and which will bring success in today's dramatically changing, competitive marketplace. Or not.

strategic realignment noun
1. a corporate shake-up with an eye on some future goal. 2. firing employees who are not "aligned" with the company's new strategy.

strategize *verb*
to think deeply about the future with the aim of devising a cunning plan to outsmart competitors/colleagues/etc.

streamline *verb*
1. to trim fat from an organization to make it leaner, and meaner. 2. to trim employees who have been deemed surplus to requirements.

streamlined *adjective*
1. of a sleek and honed organization, ready to slice through the competition like a knife through warm butter, or a tycoon's yacht through a flotilla of children's dinghies. 2. of an employee deemed surplus to requirements, as in, "There go the **streamlined** executives from sales and marketing."

stretching the envelope *verb*
to boldly go where no organization has gone before; to "see what you're made of"; to take it to "the edge."

sub-prime *adjective*
1. of worthless junk. 2. of loans made to those who clearly cannot or will not pay them back, with the intention of repackaging and spreading the risk across the entire financial system. 3. toxic.

supply chain *noun*
a co-ordinated system of organizations, people, activities, information, and resources involved in moving a **product** or service in physical or virtual manner from supplier to **customer**. A chain is only ever as strong as its weakest link and there'll be a weak link somewhere in that chain, take it from me.

sustainable *adjective*
1. of a state that can be maintained at a certain level indefinitely. 2. a relatively new word in the lexicon of business weasel-words as companies claim **sustainability** for any

number of processes and **products** which, in fact, require a good few planets' worth of resources.

SWOT analysis *noun cf.* **out-of-the-box**
1. the analysis of Strengths, Weaknesses, Opportunities and Threats, a favourite checklist of management trainee courses. 2. thinking decidedly *inside* the box.

syndicate *verb*
to sell something to smaller or geographically far apart institutions in order to cover a larger area in terms of population, as in, "There may not be a very big market for our **product** right here, but if we **syndicate** it, we'll be laughing all the way to the bank."

synergize *verb*
two or more agents working together to produce a result not obtainable by any of the agents independently – think raptors in *Jurassic Park*.

synergistic *adjective*
1. of incomprehensible business plans put forward by twenty-somethings, for example, "This is a **synergistic network** opportunity for the post-iPod generation." 2. of **synergy**, for example, in a company which sells both donuts and weight-loss **products**.

synergy *noun*
1. the interaction of two or more agents or forces so that their combined effect is greater than the sum of their individual effects. 2. co-operative interaction among groups, especially among the acquired subsidiaries or merged parts of a corporation, creating a gloriously enhanced, world-beating effect.

synthesize *verb*
to bring together a jumble of nonsense and try to make sense with it – a synthesizer, a popular musical instrument in the 1980s, did largely the same thing.

systemize *verb*
to devise a system which will miraculously distil order from chaos in one's life and work, as in, "There's no point in being at loggerheads with the corporation; I'm going to **systemize** myself to become one with it so I can be at peace."

systems management
1. enterprise-wide administration of computer systems. 2. what techies do. 3. cybersnooping.

T

take it offline *verb*
1. turn it off. 2. do something in secret, either because it is of questionable morality, or because you want to be able to avoid responsibilty when it goes wrong.

taking ownership *verb*
1. receiving something one has bought – taking delivery of a new car, for example. 2. buying into something; resigning yourself to the fact that there is a new **paradigm** at work and you'll be held accountable whether you give credence to the latest wave of management theory gibberish or not.

target audience *noun*
1. the kind of people that a company would like to browbeat into buying their useless **product**. 2. a stereo-typically defined section of the population about whom advertizers make patronizing assumptions.

team building
1. awkward lunchtime social gatherings of workmates with nothing in common. 2. hellish weekends away with workmates, climbing walls, canoeing, and drinking excessively to cope with the sheer boredom, much favoured by macho bosses and corporations who don't believe you are entitled to a private life outside of work.

team player *noun*
someone first in the queue to go on a team-building jaunt such as paintballing, but more usually to be found hiding behind a fug of witless bonhomie, stealthily benefiting from the hard work of colleagues.

tech-heavy Nasdaq *noun*
is there another Nasdaq that we haven't been told about?

technopeasant *noun*
an individual not well versed in the most recent technological advances.

telephonic communication *noun*
using the phone.

think outside the box *verb*
1. think creatively without regard to the "box" of rules and conventions which inhibit creative thought (Dr Edward de Bono pioneered lateral thinking as one form of **thinking outside the box**). 2. don't think, just say the first thing that comes into your head; nothing put forward by anyone having been asked to **think outside the box** will ever be acted on, so there is little risk of any terrible consequences.

third-generation contingencies *noun*
things that might go wrong, but not until years in the future, by which time you'll hopefully be far away and beyond the reach of blame.

ticks in boxes, putting
1. following a procedure in an unthinking, mechanical way. 2. doing everything by the book, regardless of whether you are achieving anything or not. 3. covering your ass.

timeline *noun*
1. the order in which things will occur and how long they will take. 2. hurry up, as in, "Can you give me a **timeline** on that?"

time to market *noun*
the length of time between a **product** being conceived and being available for sale; companies generally attempt to strike a balance between cutting important, and expensive, stages in the development process in order to beat their competitors to market and producing complete crap, not always entirely successfully.

title inflation
the lengthening of job titles as an organization grows. Effectiveness in a particular role is generally in inverse proportion to the length of a title, i.e., the more pompous and long-winded a title, the less effective the person doing the job (this holds true particularly with regard to qualifying terms such as "associate" or "senior").

top-down *adjective*
of management telling employees what to do, and employees doing it.

total quality
1. excellence in every aspect or stage of a process, no matter how insignificant it might seem, in order to ensure the quality of the end **product**. 2. patchy rubbish.

touch base *verb*
to talk to someone to discover what is going on in their job, their life; although it sounds inconsequential and friendly, it can have an undertone of menace, as in, "I think I need to **touch base** with you on the Simpson Project, I'm concerned that things are beginning to slide."

traction *noun*
attracting power or influence, as in, "Have you noticed Gonzalez? He's starting to gain some **traction** within the company."

trailblazing
showing the way; making a path for others to follow; doing something that has not been done before (perhaps because no one, quite rightly, had thought it worthwhile).

transform *verb*
to change one thing into something else, like privatizing a state department and turning it into a **service-oriented** public company, or using a sow's ear to make a silk purse.

transition *verb*
to change from one thing into another, as in, "You seem to be struggling to **transition** from sales assistant into manager so I'm going to have to let you go."

tune in *verb*
1. to accustom yourself to hearing the dog whistles of management and responding appropriately. 2. to try to lower yourself to the level of your colleagues so that you can understand them.

turnkey *adjective*
fully equipped, ready to go into operation immediately, as in, "No, really, it's a **turnkey** business, **oven-ready**. Now, if you'll just sign here, here, and here, please."

U

unleash *verb*
to set free some pent up force, as in, "Unleash your inner entrepreneur!" Advertizers are particularly fond of the word, employing it in bathetic appeals such as, "Unleash the cleaning power of new KleenCream for a sparkling-clean kitchen!"

unleashing the visionary
thinking outside the box, as in, "I think my approach up till now has been too plodding and unimaginative; I've been thinking of **unleashing the visionary**."

unsung hero *noun*
the Stakhanovite in the office, slaving away unrewarded; not celebrated in ballads or praise poems, but the man or woman on whose shoulders rests the success or failure of an entire enterprise.

upgrade *noun*
computer science an "improvement" to hardware or software, often involving an unfeasible and unworkable number of new features, none of them wanted.

up-sell *verb*
to attempt to have the consumer purchase more expensive items, upgrades, or other add-ons in an attempt to make a more profitable sale (a bullying technique of questionable legality to persuade a consumer to pay for extras that he or she does not want).

upskill *verb*
to learn additional skills, as in, "She started as a shelf stacker, but since then she has constantly **upskilled** and is now the branch manager."

urgency, a sense of *noun*
1. a feeling that one is rushing to achieve something. 2. the impression that one is rushing to achieve something, all quick hand movements, earnest expressions, and bluster – the appearance demanded of workers that they should seem to care. 3. walking very rapidly around the office, in an attempt to convey one's importance.

user-centric *adjective*
impossible to use.

USP *noun*
1. Unique Selling Point: a quality dreamt up by the marketing department, hyped by the sales team, but totally unrelated to any aspect of the actual **product**. 2. a fiction intended to intimidate and confuse consumers.

utilize *verb*

to use . . . anything . . . anyone to achieve the results you want.

V

validate *verb*
to try to make something satisfy certain criteria that are made up by the manufacturers anyway, so essentially meaningless, as in, "It does what it says it does because we say what it does."

value
what **products** used to have before corporations wised up.

value-added *adjective*
corporate-speak for making a **product** more expensive by some obscure improvement/modification which makes it seem better value for money. Look carefully, and you'll see that it's not.

value chain *noun*
a chain of activities through which a **product** passes, gaining in value at each stage; the chain gives the product more added value than the sum of added values of each

activity, e.g., liposuction, cosmetic surgery, tooth veneers, hair extensions, fake tan, designer dress, designer shoes . . .

vertical *adjective*
upright.

vertical merger *noun*
1. a merger in which a company acquires its suppliers or **customers**, with the result that costs are reduced and the **customer** gets a better deal (*archaic*). 2. a brutal buy-out in which a company solves its supplier or **customer** problems by buying them and running them into the ground. 3. the acquisition of a company which one has no idea how to run.

vice-president *noun*
a corporate drone who accepted a fancy job title instead of a pay rise.

videoblog *noun*
a badly made home video uploaded onto the internet for no apparent reason.

viral *adjective*
of objects or patterns able to replicate themselves or convert other objects into copies of themselves when these objects are exposed to them.

viral marketing *noun*
the use of techniques such as infiltrating **blogs** and forums and hiring actors to go to trendy bars to promote a **product**; the idea is that the promotion will become self-replicating: people will forward amusing clips, or tell their friends how great a product is because they saw a certain

celebrity using it in a particular club. Marketing as disease.

vision *noun*
1. sight. 2. a mental image of the glorious sunlit uplands of a company's future; what the boss, alone on a rocky outcrop, sees: the promised land, where the buildings are made of bars of precious metals and the louvre blinds are made from banknotes.

visualize *verb*
to create a mental picture; to envisage the future as you wish it to be; for your position in the company within five years to be as tangible as if you were already earning that salary, driving that car, sitting in that corner office.

vortal *noun*
a website which provides information and resources for a particular industry, typically providing news, research and statistics, discussions, newsletters, and many other services to educate users about a specific industry; almost as good for work avoidance as meetings – hours can be whiled away "keeping up to speed" with developments in your industry.

walk the talk *verb*
1. the opposite of "all mouth and no trousers"; doing, not just saying; a phrase used by macho business guys to imply that not only do they talk like uncaring jerks, but that they are also capable of behaving like uncaring jerks. 2. to do what you said you would do, as in, "I've shared the **vision**, now let's **walk the talk**."

war chest *noun*
1. cash set aside by the company for future acquisitions or unanticipated emergencies. 2. money for a campaign, political or otherwise; the wherewithal to wage war, as in, "In order to finance their acquisitions hitlist they had amassed a huge **war chest**."

watercooler game *noun*
a videogame intended to serve some purpose in advertising, politics, or anywhere else beyond the sphere of entertainment; games that will hopefully result in discussion

"around the watercooler," for example, a whack-a-mole game to focus attention on a particular politician's problems with leaks from his office.

web-readiness *noun*
the state of preparedness of a company for doing business on the Web. As Machiavelli wrote, over five hundred years ago, "The one who adapts his policy to the times prospers, and likewise the one whose policy clashes with the demands of the times does not."

whiteboard *verb*
1. to share files on-screen; a form of videoconferencing enabling users to mark up a whiteboard in much the same way as they would a wall-mounted whiteboard. 2. to treat employees like schoolchildren.

white-rat *verb*
to try out an idea, as in, "I'm not sure that would work, but why don't you put together a team and **white-rat** it."

wild goose chase
see **runaround**.

wingman *noun*
someone in a supportive role, looking out for and protecting a colleague – a borrowing from the high-flying, macho world of films such as *Top Gun*.

win-win *noun*
a situation which allows all parties to succeed to a degree.

win-win *adjective*
1. mutually beneficial. 2. a double-whammy for one side and a crushing victory for the other. 3. a complete triumph. 4. a flimsily disguised swindle, wherein what is given with one hand is taken tenfold with the other.

work *verb*
exertion or effort directed to produce or accomplish something; labour; toil.

work *noun*
1. something on which exertion or labour is expended; a task or undertaking. 2. time spent whiling away the day, doing nothing particularly useful; a way of frittering away one's life more or less completely fruitlessly (not to be confused with "life's work").

work-based training
training to work more effectively by working less effectively because of interruptions caused by training.

world-class *adjective*
barely competent.

wow factor *noun*
the qualities of a **product** that make the consumer say "Wow!" as in "Wow! This new noodle-based chocolate drink is unbelievably awful!" or "Wow, my car's engine just spontaneously burst into flames!"

Even More Bullshit Job Titles

Generate your own bullshit job title, or help someone else with theirs. Simply combine one word, chosen randomly, from each column to generate a new title.

Lead	Creative	Supervisor
Senior	Configuration	Associate
Direct	Accountability	Executive
Corporate	Interactions	Liaison
Dynamic	Research	Officer
Future	Factors	Manager
Product	Directives	Engineer
National	Usability	Specialist
Regional	Integration	Director
District	Metrics	Co-ordinator

Xcellence
Oh, puh-leese . . .

X-Factor
a bit like the **wow factor**, but more geared to Hollywood,
A-list style inanity.

X, Generation . . .
the **target audience** for a wide variety of inane **products**.

Xtra *adjective*
adspeak for extra, as in, "It's not really an extra, but if we
spell it wrong, we can't be sued, right?"

Y

yes-man/men *noun*
an employee/employees whose primary role is to agree
with any hare-brained scheme dreamt up by his/their boss.

yesterday's news
1. any mistake that the boss ever made – don't ever
mention it if you want to survive. 2. the status of a
formerly favoured employee whose project crashed and
burned.

your call
1. you make the decision, and take the inevitable flak for
it. 2. on your own head be it. 3. I haven't got the faintest
idea what to do, yet by letting you make the decision I
look magnanimous.

Z

zero-sum game
in game theory, a situation in which a participant's gain or loss is exactly balanced by the losses or gains of the other participant(s), for example, it is possible for only one player to win a game of chess – the other player loses. Situations in which all participants can benefit or lose together, for example, one country with a rice surplus trading with another with a grain surplus, is a **non-zero-sum-game**. "It's not a **zero-sum game**; we can 'grow the pie' to benefit everyone" is a favourite business maxim, though how often it is true is a moot point.

Z-list *adjective*
the status of any celebrity cheap enough to endorse your company's **product**.

zone, in the

where bragging **salespeople** claim to be following a successful sale. **Salespeople** are like gamblers in that they only remember their last conspicuous success.

zoo, the *noun*

1. what the sales team call the creative team. 2. what the creative team call the sales team. 3. what the production department call the entire company.

Bullshit Builder I

Combine one word or phrase from each column to craft your own piece of incomprehensible bullshit.

Their	inaccurate	feedback	inflates our	entry level
My	debit-impaired	department	radicalizes the	balance sheet
This	unsupported	content	leads us to the	earnings
A future	aggregate	guesstimate	minimises the	income statement
A/An	auditable	post maker	increases our	statement of cash flows
The	reviewable	reverse asset	underlies the	owner's equity
A new	attestable	enter box	actions the	unsold assets
Which	traceable	bill surrender	shakes up our	liability
Our	material	estimate yield	escalates out	common stock
Any	immaterial	basis	realigns our	preferred stock

Bullshit Builder II

Combine one word or phrase from each column to craft your own piece of incomprehensible bullshit.

Let's run the	goodwill	onto the runway	and cash in the	accounts receivable
Take the	notes receivable	up the flagpole	to fully equip the	equity
We can force the	franchise	past the accounts team	so as to reamortize the the	marketable securities
R&D will move the	patent	to the bank	without fail for the	product launch
We'll action the	accounts payable	onto the bottom line	in time for the	viral marketing campaign
The PR team are to push the	bond issue	cut to the chase	not forgetting the	compulsory upgrade
The CEO wants to see the	loan	onto the grindstone	so we can focus on the	office seating reorganization

Bullshit Builder III

Combine one word or phrase from each column to craft your own piece of incomprehensible bullshit.

We must understand the	watercooler games	instead of the	prospective	stock options
Look to the	treasury stock	as well as the	preliminary	double entries
Don't forget the	brain dump	in spite of the	disclaimed	selling points
First, let's look at the	low-hanging fruit	that follows the	unqualifed	blue-sky ideas
So that we're on the same page, here's the	bandwidth	within the remit of the	unaccrued	synergistic schemes
From a customer-centric viewpoint, remember the	bond issue	cut to the chase	not forgetting the	get-out clauses
No need to reinvent the	solution	within the	adverse	redundancies

Bullshit Builder IV

Combine one word or phrase from each column to craft your own piece of incomprehensible bullshit.

Let's take it offline	networking	issues	create the	personnel redeployment
At the end of the day	accountability management	benefits	point to the	knowledge base
Thinking outside the box	core competency	details	allow a/an	win-win scenario
I hear what you say	risk management	ballpark	fund a/an	performance indicator
Taking the big picture	empowerment	solutions	revisit the	attitude realignment
24/7	blame culture	synergy	suggest a/an	incremental approach
In best practice	differential	paradigms	are the	new metrics

Bullshit Builder V

Combine one word or phrase from each column to craft your own piece of incomprehensible bullshit.

We have a/an	authentic	core business plan in	the next millennium
We are working towards the	focus-group approved	perfect market in	human advancement
Imagine a/an	quality	benchmark in	marketable junk
I can attest to a/an	previously unheard of	turning point for	the Internet 3.0
We are proposing a/an	top of the range	personalized product for	life, liberty and happiness
I can unveil the	completely safety-tested	legal Ponzi scheme for	the replacement of human imagination
Have you ever wanted a/an	idiotproof	child's toy for	the globalized workforce

The Art of Sales Bullshit

A psychopath is defined as someone who uses charm, manipulation, intimidation, and violence to control others and to satisfy their own needs. If you leave out the violence this is more or less a definition of the ideal personality for the role of salesperson. And most sales-people would consider violence if they couldn't find another way to close a sale.

Like politicians, salespeople are accomplished liars. In fact, they are so accomplished, they often persuade themselves that what they are saying is actually true. As a result it becomes very difficult to tell when a salesperson is lying to you. However, if you are familiar with the basic art of sales bullshit, then you can occasionally see through the patter and catch a dim glimpse of the truth. It sometimes helps to look at the salesperson and remember that this is someone who is one wrestling move away from a dangerous psychiatric disorder.

The first thing to bear in mind with all salespeople is that all that matters to them is clinching the deal. The first commandment of sales is ABC, which stands for "Always Be Closing." This means that from the moment they start talking to you (the customer) they are aiming towards this one conclusion, closing the deal. If they are chatting to you, this is merely to butter you up to make you think favourably of them. Because, if you like them, you will be more likely to buy their product. Any friendly question they ask you is merely a tactical manoeuvre in the game of closing the deal.

Obviously there are all sorts of salespeople in the world, selling all kinds of different products. But there are many strategies that they share. The first thing the salesperson needs to do is to establish why you need or want their product. They will attempt to pinpoint a Unique Selling Point, and to commit you to needing a product with that USP. For instance, if a telesales agent is trying to persuade you to take out a credit card that you don't need, they will play up the advantages of the extremely short honeymoon period in which the rates are unnaturally low. Of course the rates will be set so as to shoot up to an unnaturally high level thereafter to compensate. Companies hate to actually offer you a good deal, so always compensate for any "special offer" with a punishing, excessive charge somewhere else. A half-price bathroom from the home store will come with a double-price fitting charge. A free three-month subscription will come with an overpriced subsequent nine months, plus the company will be aiming to sell your personal details to any Tom, Dick, or Harry who wants to pester you in the privacy of your home.

On one level, the salesman knows that the USP or special offer he is plugging is worthless. But on another level he doesn't care. All he needs to do is to get you to sign on the dotted line, so that he can move on to the next victim. If you are hesitant, there are various bullshit weapons that can be deployed. The first is the arbitrary deadline. The salesman will offer to hold a product or deal for you for a limited period only. If you don't make your mind up by 5 p.m., or by a week Tuesday, this once-in-a-lifetime opportunity will be lost. Salesmen love deadlines, it is one of the ways they attempt to intimidate and manipulate you. The best response to this is to immediately undermine the deadline. For instance, if he tells you that you have to decide by the end of the day, say that you are going to be undergoing mild surgery that afternoon, and that if he can't wait longer, you'll have to say no. Usually this will force him into extending his deadline, at which point you will know that it was bullshit in the first place.

The next intimidation strategy deployed by sales people is the threat that someone else will buy this product if you don't commit. Clothes shops do this by leaving only one size of each item of each style on the racks. They have a huge pile of each item out the back of the store. But if there is only one item your size on show, you feel under pressure to make a decision. You decide to carry the item around the store with you, just in case someone else takes your beautiful shirt or trousers. In your mind you have already succumbed to the sales bullshit.

Realtors (estate agents) have a different box of tools. They will deliberately arrange to show a property to several different parties at the same time in order to create the feeling of an auction. While you are all milling around the same tiny condo eyeing each other up they will take a phone call, and tell you that they have already received an offer on the property. In fact the phone call was a pre-arranged one from a bored colleague in the office, for the purpose of putting the fear of God in you that if you don't leap into a bid for this overpriced hellhole then you will have missed the boat. It's perfectly possible that the other "interested buyers" milling around the property are also stooges, employees who are in on the scam. It's no coincidence that many confidence tricksters got their start as sales people.

Salespeople love to convey the idea of missing the boat, or the train or whatever. They'll say to you, "Jump on the train or get run down," or, "Don't miss the boat," or, "The plane is revving up, the pilot is waiting." All of these metaphors key into our deep-seated fears, reminding us of those anxiety dreams we have at night where we are running from one place to another missing our connections. And anxiety is the saleman's friend.

So the salesman has managed to charm you into liking him and wanting to do business with him. He has persuaded you that his product is unique. He has managed to scare you into thinking that you have to make a quick decision, because he knows that most bad decisions are the ones made on the spur of the moment. Now he just needs to make it easier for you to say yes than to say no. At this point you will notice his patter becomes especially intense and repetitive. Like a snake hypnotizing its prey, he is closing in on that mythical deal. He is trying to lull you into a sense of trust and security while at the same time making it hard for you to get out of the conversation without a commitment. He will remind you that you have a period in which you can cancel so you are not really committing. He will offer new credit terms under which you pay only a few dollars a month (although on closer examination this deal will be for the rest of your living days and any shorter payment period will be painfully expensive). He will throw in spurious extras – this car comes with an extra steering wheel, that credit card comes with worthless insurance which will pay out under no circumstances known to science. All this is just an attempt to bamboozle you into that final decision. Always Be Closing.

This is your big moment. Look that salesperson in the eye, gather your courage and reach down deep inside you for one simple word, "No!".

If you really want to buy something, then go away and quietly think about it without a salesperson yapping in your ear. You may decide you still want it, but never say yes under the pressure of a sales pitch. You will hate yourself later when you realize that you committed to buying some piece of overpriced trash for a ludicrous price.

Remember, the first commandment of being a customer – "Just Say No."

The Art of Mission Statement Bullshit

Discretion prevents us from revealing which major company came up with the following as an early draft of their extended mission statement. Suffice it to say that this version was later dropped as being too truthful, and replaced with something even more sinister. This company's bullshit is fairly representative of most company's goals. If you ever need to write your own firm a mission statement, you could do worse than boil this down into its constituent parts:

Our Mission Statement
"To Own the World and Make It Pay"

We strive to efficiently enhance innovative benefits so that we may collaboratively leverage existing seven-habits-conforming leadership skills in order to solve business problems. Yes, we will stop at nothing to give you complete customer satisfaction, even if you do not use our products. We are here to please you whether you want it or not. We fully intend to be completely in your face on television, morning, noon and night. We shall publish our mission statement in every newspaper and magazine that you may buy. Our jingles will haunt your dreams.

Our challenge is to globally initiate principle-centered leadership skills while continuing to conveniently co-ordinate mission-critical content for 100% customer satisfaction. We fully intend to rule your world. You will not be allowed to ignore our intentions – it is our mission to globally utilize progressive leadership skills while appearing on the back of your cereal box.

We scout profitable growth opportunities in relationships, both internally and externally. The power to achieve the life of your dreams is in our hands. We make it our business to know where you are going. We intend to explore new paradigms and then filter and communicate and evangelize the findings in the most boring way possible. We can professionally co-ordinate unique intellectual capital to allow us to globally create diverse sources of bullshit material. We have already proved ourselves more cut-throat than the competition and we are determined to monopolize emerging inclusive markets.

The first step toward activating you is identifying the specific goals that will make our dreams reality. We have committed to quickly co-ordinate interdependent catalysts for change so that we may globally provide access to world-class leadership skills to set us apart from the competition. After all, it's much easier to get what we want out of life when we know where you're going. That's where our satellite-tracking arm will come in useful.

We exist to globally administrate scalable paradigms to allow us to proactively customize emerging sources to work for our benefit while you eat your breakfast. It is our job to competently co-ordinate a few competitive benefits to meet our customers' needs and desires even while washing their hair.

We have committed to synergistically customize timely information to make us appear the only option when waiting for a bus. We are certain that our services can count on you to professionally pursue multimedia-based technology in order that we may globally restore virtual data to meet our customers' needs. There is no more need for telephone directories or libraries. We envision to continually engineer leadership skills while continuing to collaboratively revolutionize enterprise-wide opportunities in order to solve business problems.

We have already identified that we need to continue to proactively negotiate low-risk high-yield infrastructures in order that we may enthusiastically engineer value-added paradigms while maintaining the highest standards of fatuousness. It is our responsibility to synergistically supply principle-centred products while continuing to quickly foster cost effective technology and world domination. We can guarantee to completely administrate all leadership skills to set us apart from the rest of the bloodsuckers. We envision to interactively co-ordinate prospective materials in a way that is nauseating and useless to all but the brain dead.

Finally, we have made a commitment to seamlessly simplify all information to prevent independent thought and to collaboratively facilitate interdependent people with endlessly meaningless mission statements. After all, we have made it our business to poke our noses into your business because we know that is what the customer expects.

The Art of Interview Bullshit

Interviews are intended to find out if you've lied on your CV. Before you attend the interview, read your CV and remember what you wrote. The interviewer/s will ask you about it. Have a last check of the information you have given the potential employer so you are ready to back up your claims with facts and examples. Have your notebook to hand if you want to use one.

Don't fall at the first hurdle – unfortunately you do have to be on time (even if it's only this once). Be at the "start line" early and memorize the route if necessary. For some companies, how smartly you are dressed is more important than whether or not you can actually do the job. Of course you know this is stupid but humour them anyway – having power over the way you have to look is just one more screw in the coffin of independence that the corporate world demands. Perhaps a coffee will ease the nerves; but alcohol is out and even the smell of nicotine may do little for your cause in the eyes of this demanding militia.

When you arrive, the receptionist may try to exert a little power over you, first, by completely ignoring you, and then by behaving as if you are of no importance and showing you the way to the interview room with a dismissive attitude. Maintain a pleasant disposition – remind yourself that if you get the job you can get your revenge by inviting everyone to lunch but her or refusing to say "good morning" when you arrive. You will be asked to wait and wait. This is quite literally a test of patience so it is in your interest to remain positive. They are trying to break you before you've even got started so dig in, no matter how far the clock gets beyond the appointment time – do not allow their mind games to unsettle you. Just keep the notion of revenge in your head, visit the bathroom to do a little deep breathing if you need to, and keep cheerful.

When you walk into the room, shake hands regardless of the idiotic demons in suits that sit facing you. They expect you to wait until asked to sit like a nervous eleven-year-old on his or her first day at junior school. Grit your teeth and wait. If they give you the job you can sit with your feet on the desk for the rest of the year. They will probably stare at you as if they're wondering what species you are. Maintain eye contact without being threatening, and speak normally. This is the point where you have to back up your CV with interesting information. As well as your personal qualities, skills, competencies, qualifications and experience, you must show that you are enthusiastic about both the job and the organization. They want someone who is committed and keen. If you are neither you must act the part anyway. No job will be given without at least a little participation from you.

Often, one of the first questions will be, "What did you like best and least about your last job?" Beware, this is always a trick question. You know, and they know, that you left your last job because you hated it, otherwise why are you applying for another? Do not say this. Give specific examples of how your last job allowed you to flex your skills and show your maturity (leave out the fact that they made you do everything and shouted at you like a naughty child). When answering the bit about what you liked least, keep it short, do not be negative, and relate your answer to how your last job limited you in your ability to exhibit strong leadership qualities. Take care not to give the impression that you are someone who will threaten their positions or upset their workforce, so do not act like an army commander, constantly issuing orders. Even if it is not your intention, you are likely to conjure up dangerous media images from war films.

You may also be asked what you have learned from your mistakes. This is another tricky one. Do not say that you have never made any mistakes – they will know that you are lying. The trick is to concentrate on the positive aspect of the question to do with "learning" rather than on the negative aspect to do with "mistakes." Do not tell them that most of your previous customers were jerks and you stopped talking to them when they were angry by putting all your calls to voicemail or unplugging your phone. Say something like, "I have had one or two hiccups with customers where their satisfaction was not what it might have been. I learned to monitor certain customers and their needs closely and to 'take their temperature' so that I could keep their satisfaction level as high as possible. Have you had any customers like that here?" You have to spot the traps in every question. Never answer a question truthfully – they just want you to tell them what an ideal, superhuman person would do when faced with wailing idiots.

They may ask you to describe a situation when working
with a team produced more successful results than if you
had completed the project on your own. You know that
working as a team is always a hindrance because you have
to take into account so many different egos, and put your
trust in so many idiots. This is what is called a "behavioural interviewing" style of question. The interview
panel wants to learn more about your thought processes.
You need to show your ability to solicit ideas from others,
listen carefully, and persuade people to adopt your point
of view, but without being an overbearing monster. You
don't want to make them afraid of you . . . yet. Say
something like, "Working with others has often yielded
great results for projects I have been involved in – specif-
ically when it came to brainstorming. I try to get everyone
involved in coming up with new solutions by making time
for sessions where there are no wrong ideas or answers.
The creativity of a group of people is always going to be
greater than that of any one individual." Yes, utter
rubbish, very necessary, unfortunately, if you want the
job.

They may ask you at the end of the interview to tell
them anything else that is relevant to your job application.
What you must put across is what you can do for them. It
is the employer's needs that must be addressed, not your
wishes. This is not the time for false modesty so try
something like, "Mr Big Boots, just before we wrap up
here, I want to ask you to put your faith in me and give me
the job. I will reward you by doing my absolute best to do
quality work and make our department shine."

After leaving the interview room, remember to make it
out of sight before burying your head in your hands and
wondering if you even want their stupid job at all. If you
choose to go to a bar and drink away the shame and lies,

then remember not to use the bar right next door to your prospective employers. The last thing you need is to run into one of your interviewers after three hours of non-stop drinking and let them know exactly what you think of them and their company.

Last, but not least, good luck! You'll need it.

The Art of Body-Language Bullshit

You may feel, if your colleagues are bandying about bullshit buzzwords in lieu of actually communicating with you, that you will be able to rumble them through your grasp of body language. After all, you may reason, body language can comprise 50 per cent of what we are saying. However, that is to discount Body-Language Bullshit. Yes, it's not just with their lying lips that your colleagues, clients, suppliers, and competitors are trying to bamboozle you, but with their faces and bodies, too.

When analysing body language, it is important to take account of "clusters" (*groups* of gestures and expressions). The same is true of analysing Body-Language Bullshit. Those skilled in using their faces and bodies to get one over you will be well versed in consciously deploying "clusters" to mislead you as to what they are really feeling or thinking, but occasionally – and this is the chink in their armour – there will be so-called "cluster dissonance." By spotting anomalies in the gestures and expressions being feigned, you will be able to pick apart the bullshitters' attempts to dissemble. For example, someone may assume a seemingly disingenuous "open" posture – arms and legs open rather than folded or crossed and so on – but a telltale twitching of an eyelid, or a muscle in their jaw, could betray real tension. You may, in fact, have them on the ropes; alternatively they may be attempting to lure you into an attack only to ambush you. At least you will not have been lulled into a false sense of security.

Body-Language Bullshitters (BLBs) will aim, in every conceivable way, to be "higher" than you. They will stand taller, sit on a higher chair, or on a raised platform, stand over you while you sit, and so on. Female BLBs wear high heels (some men, too, wear so-called "Cuban" heels, or lifts) and both male and female BLBs will drive conspicuously "higher" cars (unless they're in expensive sports cars and therefore *lower* than everyone else). Still, they have distinguished themselves in one way or another. You, on the other hand, are likely to be driving a mere mid-height, middle-of-the-road car; they're not, and therein lies the difference.

Aggression is signalled by frowns, pursed lips, or, in more extreme situations, sneers and snarls. Someone on the point of attacking you in a business environment is likely to have clenched fists, a lowered body posture (as if braced for a fight) and a slight or pronounced reddening of the face. But all of this, even the facial flush, could be faked, perhaps in an attempt to bully you into signing a contract, buying something, or just giving in on some point or another. Look for contradictory signals, such as dry lips (being licked slightly too often), a tell-tale trembling lip, the avoidance of eye contact. Now you can safely ignore the too blatant display of aggression and insist on changes to the contract, or send the sales person packing, or simply stand up to your boss, not having meekly succumbed to fear in the face of a false threat.

Deploy some Body-Language Bullshit yourself. Provoke someone to lose his or her cool by looking away, by displaying your crotch to them (spreading your legs and perhaps even pointing at your genitalia), by moving into their space, uninvited, to show them who's boss. Once you have them rattled, move swiftly to take advantage of their discomposure.

Let's face it, all too often at work we are bored out of our wits. But it doesn't do to show this, particularly in certain situations. So how does one feign interest, in situations when one really should at least look as if one cares? Perhaps you're having a meal with your boss, listening to a cruelly dull account of their deeply tedious and uneventful life, utterly devoid of purpose. The way to get her to imagine that you're listening – that you care – is to do the following:

• Appear to ignore distractions. This may be difficult at first, but practise at home – with a ringing phone, your spouse or children calling, a dog barking, the doorbell buzzing.

• Keep still: don't fidget. Again, not easy to get right at first, but retreat into yourself and find the Zen-like calm that you need to still all movement, or as much of it as you can.

• Lean forward: not so far as to seem to be about to topple off your chair, but sufficiently far forward to appear interested, say 30 degrees.

- Tilt your head: not so much as to appear to have cricked your neck – just a slight tilt away from the vertical will impress on your boss that you are agog, waiting expectantly for her next juicy morsel of conversation.

- Keep your gaze steady and level. Look at her with feigned fascination. Try to keep your blink rate down, though try, too, not to open your eyes too wide – a relaxed, consistent gaze is what you're aiming for.

- Furrow your brow – slightly. You don't want to appear angry, or baffled, but you do want to appear to be concentrating, hanging on her every word.

- "Open" your body. Don't sit there with your arms tightly folded, hunched over your crossed legs, but spread your arms, spread your legs, appear to invite further confidences with every part of your body.

- Nod slowly, not so much as to appear to be nodding off, but gravely, compassionately. You are listening, you are hearing, you understand, and you care.

- Make "interest noises," for example, "Uh huh," "Ah" and so on: little grunts of assent and comprehension. Again, be wary of seeming to snore or to be asleep, or incapable of speech. These little grunts of interest should generally follow the conclusion of some passage, rather than being deployed randomly interrupting the flow of your boss's soliloquy. If you're not actually listening, you can pick up on falling cadences which will give you an indication of when might be an appropriate moment to give a little grunt.

- "Reflect" your boss. Mirror her body language and paraphrase what she is saying. Obviously this would be extraordinarily irritating if taken to extremes: copying each gesture exactly and parroting whatever she says. Instead, subtly rearrange your posture to match hers, repeat little snatches of what is being said to you, perhaps along with little grunts of assent.

If you can keep up this veneer of seeming interest, your mind behind the veil, as it were, is free to roam. Initially it will be difficult to function in parallel, but surprisingly quickly it will begin to come naturally to you. You will find it possible to attend meetings, even one-on-one meetings with colleagues, underlings, superiors, your boss, or clients and seem to be giving them valuable "face time" while really your mind is occupied with making mental to-do lists, visualizing the upcoming weekend, or a past holiday, or composing letters, e-mails, and memos. This is not so much multi-tasking as putting up an effective, even winning, screen behind which you can get on with what really matters: looking after number one.

The Art of Retail Bullshit

The first commandment of retail bullshit is, "Make people come and buy from your store." Appearance is everything in pursuit of this goal. Play innocuous-sounding muzak containing subliminal messages to brainwash consumers into thinking that they really do need a new pink plasma television and a zebra-skin rug. Even if you've got only a few items to sell, you need to give the appearance of a fully stocked shop, even when it is not. The usual trick is to put the best of your stock in the window or near the front of the store. This will help to draw people in even if everything which is not in the windows or close to the front is shop-soiled tat – or groceries decidedly past their prime, if you're in the food line.

Think design space! You want people to see your shop as a calm, hassle-free shopping environment even if there is often little space to manouevre between the shelves or rails and the aisles are full of people clutching full baskets continually crashing into each other. They're in your shop . . . you've achieved something: you're on your way to being a proper retailer. Of course, you don't really want people lingering now; you need them to buy something, or plenty of things, and then go away. Design a space that draws them in and makes your products appear so enticing that it's hard for customers to leave without shovelling their cash at you. The ideal shop lures its customers in, bewilders them into buying something, and swiftly and unceremoniously dumps them back on to the street, wondering what the hell they just did.

If you're running a large chain of retail shops, the trick is to make each shop identical. Consumers are sheeplike in their habits and will follow the crowd if that's where the crowd is going. Stupid people feel reassured by the might of a selling institution surrounding them. One of the appeals of a large retail chain is that consumers feel comforted by the fact that many other buyers before them have also been taken in by the shiny window displays and overpriced goods. If others think the shop is good, why question it, it's probably good, right? So make your retail arena as shiny and glossy as possible – it should shimmer with appeal. People need to feel empowered; they need to believe that they have the power to buy your goods, and that buying your goods will make them more powerful. Facilitate that virtuous circle of self-belief – make it as easy as possible for them to hand over their credit or their banknotes.

Sometimes shopping is a matter of obtaining necessities such as food; sometimes it is a recreational activity. Recreational shopping often involves window shopping (just looking, not buying) and browsing, which does not always result in a purchase. Clever retailers are now onto this. Shops and stores selling non-essential goods such as clothing and jewelry are top of the list for recreational shoppers. Here, the consumer is most often a woman, sometimes accompanied by a reluctant male. The term "retail therapy" has been coined for just such an activity, and retailers love it. Retail therapy implies that by buying something you will feel better. It draws people into the shops and gets them buying things every time they encounter a problem at work, in a relationship, or just feel a bit depressed or bored. Why do you need to feel down when you could have those beautiful green shoes or that wonderful jacket? By filling their stores with ever-changing collections of covetable clothes and unneeded yet desirable items large retailers make huge profits.

Change at least some of your stock weekly to give the impression that all items are limited and must therefore be bought immediately. Of course they are not. Many retailers may rotate their stock over, say, a six-week period so it just looks as if it is constantly changing, but, really, it is just one large collection displayed in rotation. The proof of this comes with the sales when retailers just drag the whole lot out and sell it off dirt cheap. The illusion of scarcity is undone, but hopefully a lot of people will take the bait and run up crippling debts, helping the retailer to a handsome profit.

Never stop thinking about how to chisel more profit out of your customers. Most retailers source goods where they can be made very cheaply enabling them to mark them up by 500 per cent, or even 1,000 per cent. Another common technique is to use "suggested retail pricing" or a "recommended retail price"(RRP). This simply involves charging the amount suggested by the manufacturer and usually printed on the product by the manufacturer. It can also be used to advertise a sale where goods are marked down from their recommended price and sold as a supposed bargain. Remember, though, that there are plenty of goods that are never actually sold for their RRP, which is often simply an illusory high price used to make any lower price look like a bargain.

Ridiculous price discrimination is popular with any retailers who feel they can get away with it. In some shops and stores, customers may have to pay more if the seller determines that they are stupid enough to be able to afford it. Retailers may decide that their customers are stupid on the basis of their wealth, carelessness, lack of knowledge, or simply their eagerness to spend.

Retailers who have overstocked as a result of wild optimism or simple greed, usually resort to "Sales," when prices are marked down, often by a percentage – "50% off," for example. Sales are often held at fixed times of the year, for example the January sales, held after Christmas, or end-of-season sales. By reducing the price of stock gradually, from 30% off to 50% off, then 75% off, retailers allow people to think that they're getting a bargain. This is most prevalent at the high end of retail where something costing $900, say, is sold for $399. Never mind that it's just a sweater, "Look! $500 off! Bargain!" Most large retailers always make a profit, even during sales. This is largely because they buy products manufactured in a country where the average wage is $10 a month, thus ensuring a massive mark-up on goods sold in a country where the average wage is twenty times higher.

The latest retail scam is virtual shopping, through the internet or by means of mail-order catalogs. Virtual retailing does not involve the expense of running a shop or store and so can be very lucrative for the money-hungry retailer. Since you can't actually see or touch the goods, many virtual retailers use "testimonials" supposedly written by customers who have already bought goods and are blissfully happy with them. These "testimonials" are generally written by the administrative staff over their morning coffee break when they take the opportunity to tell consumers that their products are "authentic," or their services "excellent." With no travel costs, and without the hassle of walking around looking for something, consumers can buy in the safety and comfort of their own home and this gives retailers the perfect captive audience which they can milk to get people to hand over their hard-earned cash.

However, remember that most online retailers attempt to increase their profits by collecting details about their customers and either selling them to other companies or bombarding customers' e-mail inboxes with lists of other items which they sell and would like their customers to buy. Once the customer buys from an online retailer, they will never be free of that company again unless they sell their family home, throw their computer into the nearest canal or river and move into the mountains, or the desert, beyond the reach of phone lines.